Mastering New Testament Facts

| PROGRAMMED READING |
| ART AND ACTIVITIES |
| TESTS |

to get it all down PAT

BOOK 4
The General Letters and Revelation

Madeline H. Beck
Lamar Williamson, Jr.

Sketches
KATHY REAGAN
PHIL KESTNER

JOHN KNOX PRESS
Richmond, Virginia

International Standard Book Number: 0-8042-0329-6
© John Knox Press 1973
Printed in the United States of America

PREFACE

Mastering New Testament Facts is a guide for both individual and group study of the New Testament. While it has been designed for individual use, it is also easily adapted for use by study groups or classes.

Suggestions for Individual Study

The approach followed in *Mastering New Testament Facts* is one which uses recently developed learning methods. Some of these may seem to be unfamiliar at first, even though they have been used successfully both in public school education and in industry. For example, the suggestion that the student take a pre-test before he has begun to study certain chapters may seem to be an unnecessary or perhaps even an unfair step. However, it has been found that a pre-test on unfamiliar material is often helpful. Pre-tests serve to alert the student to key questions. They are basically previews which help the reader learn the material faster. All of the techniques used in this study are ways of preparing or reinforcing one's memory.

It is very important for the student to read each set of instructions carefully. If the instructions should occasionally seem to be unclear, he might wish to share his questions about them with other students or with a teacher. As this volume has not been designed as a commentary or an interpretation of the theology of the New Testament, the reader may wish to supplement it with such resources as *The Layman's Bible Commentary, The Interpreter's Bible,* a good Bible dictionary, or an atlas. *Good News for Modern Man* (Today's English Version) is the most helpful translation of the New Testament to use with *Mastering New Testament Facts.* However, other versions of the New Testament may be used if *Good News for Modern Man* is not available.

Suggestions for Group Study

There are a variety of ways in which *Mastering New Testament Facts* can be used in group study, and each group is encouraged to work out its own procedure. The following ideas may offer suggestions.

1. Each participant in the study should have his own copies of *Mastering New Testament Facts* and *Good News for Modern Man* (Today's English Version).

2. The leader or chairman should help the participants with directions in the book that might not seem to be clear.

3. Regular opportunities for individual study should be included. Thus a class may agree for the individual study to be done outside of the class time. In this case, an agreement or covenant may be adopted regarding the amount of time to be spent or the amount of material to be covered. Other groups may discover that they work best by the concentration of individual study at one class meeting and the use of alternate meeting periods for general discussion. A third approach might be to use approximately the first half of each class period for individual work and the remaining half for discussion.

4. In order to stimulate discussion, the participants could mark on scratch paper or in the margins of their New Testaments the ideas in the passage that seem to be important. A class can devise its own symbols for marking these ideas. These could be quite simple, such as E--exciting, P--puzzling, D--disturbing, H--helpful.

5. If the class is large, it might be wise to divide it into groups of fifteen or fewer for discussion.

6. The discussion may be quite informal and free flowing. On the other-hand, it could be slightly directed. Some classes may wish to discuss first the ideas which seem to be exciting or helpful; others may wish to turn to those which are troublesome as a way of beginning the discussion.

7. The interpretation of a passage of Scripture is often related to particular concerns faced by the church at critical times in its history. Thus the class may enjoy discussing the meaning of a passage for earlier generations. It may also wish to discuss the bearing a passage has on situations faced today in the church, community, or world at large.

8. If the meaning of a particular passage remains difficult to grasp, someone in the class may wish to look for additional resources or further information.

9. Ideas which may work well with one class may not work at all with another. Therefore, each class should feel free to develop its own use of the book, realizing that it should balance discussion with time for individual study.

ACKNOWLEDGMENTS

The development of this course was made possible by the generous support of the Presbyterian School of Christian Education in Richmond, Virginia. President Charles E. S. Kraemer and Dean Malcolm C. McIver, Jr., made staff time and materials available and supported the project with their interest and encouragement.

Professional readers of portions of the course included Prof. James P. Martin, Miss Gay Mothershed, Miss Peggy Ross, and Prof. Richard N. Soulen.

Volunteers for trial testing of an early draft included students at P.S.C.E., Union Theological Seminary in Virginia, Randolph-Macon College, the University of Richmond, Virginia Commonwealth University, St. Catherine's School of Richmond, and members of Westminster Presbyterian Church, Richmond, St. Thomas Episcopal Church, Richmond, and Westover Hills Presbyterian Church, Little Rock, Arkansas. Mrs. Annette Dew of Richmond worked through all four books. Comments and suggestions from these readers and volunteers contributed greatly to the present form of the course.

Typists of original drafts were Sally Lockhart and Jane E. Miller of P.S.C.E. and Mrs. Ruth K. Parrish.

To all of these collaborators in the production of this course, the authors express their deep and genuine gratitude.

CONTENTS

BEFORE YOU USE THIS BOOK . . .

You can save yourself a lot of time by reading carefully the next three pages.

Description: This study guide to the New Testament appears in four books and has been designed to help you learn the content and structure of the New Testament in the shortest possible time. The books are:

> I. *Introduction and Synoptic Gospels*
> II. *The Fourth Gospel and Acts*
> III. *The Pauline Letters*
> IV. *The General Letters and Revelation*

All four books use the PAT system (Programmed reading, Art and activities, and Tests), which enables the student to get the facts down pat.

Uses: If you do the entire course, it will prepare you to interpret any part of the New Testament in the light of all the rest. It will provide the basic acquaintance with the New Testament which is necessary for an intelligent reading of scholarly works about the New Testament. It may be particularly helpful for church school classes or Bible study groups which seek a guide to the New Testament that leaves to the student full freedom of theological interpretation and historical perspective. Newly elected church officers, church school teachers, and candidates for ordination can use this course to review New Testament content.

Any one volume of the series will serve these functions for one portion of the New Testament. Specific objectives are listed at the beginning of each unit in the course.

Learning Process: Mastery of this material proceeds through five stages--one diagnostic, and four learning and evaluative. It is the student's responsibility to see that sufficient review takes place to ensure mastery at each stage beyond the first.

Stage 1: Diagnostic Unit Pre-test

Before you begin a unit of work, you will take a pre-test to measure your present mastery of the facts and skills taught in that unit, and to become acquainted with the types of questions and information you will be learning.

While a "pre-test" may sound strange, you will soon find that it is a help to you. It's not an evaluation but a way of learning, so don't be disturbed that you do not know the material. If you already know it, you do not need to study it.

By taking a pre-test, you will understand the objectives better, you will be more alert to the kinds of information you should remember, and you will have had practice in the kinds of questions you will be using for self-evaluation later.

Then, by comparing the results of your pre-test with those of a unit test after your study, you will be able to see just how much progress you have made by studying the unit. This growth is in _knowledge_ only. The program does _not_ attempt to provide for or measure any growth in faith or development as a Christian. It is up to the individual to use this information as he thinks best.

Stage 2: Guided Reading

You will be asked to read a chapter or so at a time in the New Testament. Outline headings of each book are given in larger type, with major divisions in ALL CAPITAL LETTERS and major subheadings Initially Capitalized. Learning these headings will facilitate your memory of the content of each book and your understanding of the structure and relationship of the parts. As you read the passage under one heading and answer the questions, you will be expected to remember the heading and the major facts in that section.

Periodically you will be referred to a section chart and asked to complete a visual book outline, thereby seeing each passage in relation to the rest of the book.

As you read the passages, a series of _questions_ will call your attention to the portions of text that you need to remember. You should silently answer these questions as you read. _Answers_ appear on the back of each page of questions. It is not usually necessary for you to give the exact wording in order to be correct. These questions and answers are only to guide your study.

Sketches, which will help you remember the facts by emphasizing main ideas, accompany most answers in the guided reading. They also summarize the distinguishing features of some books at the end of the guided reading. Take time to associate the sketches with the material you have just read. They reveal more than words and are easier to recall.

Stage 3: Section Tests

Each fact, relationship, or skill that is emphasized in the guided reading or text will be tested in a section test. Section tests are organized into categories of facts to be mastered. You are given help in computing your scores for each category and for the complete test. As you complete the Unit Growth Record, you will see your progress in each area. If you score less than 90 percent on any part of the section test, you should review the relevant material in the study guide and in the New Testament.

Stage 4: Unit Test

When all sections have been completed at the 90-percent level, you are ready to begin the unit test. Once again you will be measured on your mastery of each fact, relationship, and skill taught in the sectional guided readings. You are given help in computing your scores for each category and for the entire test. By comparing your unit test score with your pre-test score you can easily determine your growth during the study of the unit.

Stage 5: Study References

Scripture references are given for all <u>unit test</u> answers. By checking the references for any items you missed on a unit test, you can complete your mastery of this unit's content. If you score less than 90 percent you should review any areas of weakness before proceeding to another unit. This does not apply if your growth from the pre-test was more than 70 percent.

NOTE: This course was designed to be used with *Good News for Modern Man: The New Testament in Today's English Version*, and its language is generally used. However, equivalent terms are used interchangeably to help you accustom yourself to terms you will meet in other books. (Examples: letter/epistle; general/catholic; mighty works/signs.)

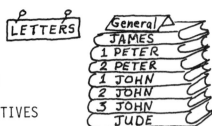

UNIT 1: THE GENERAL LETTERS

OBJECTIVES

The learnings have been classified under four major categories to help you learn more easily and to know what you are learning. The categories are: Structure, Narratives, Teachings, and Features. Upon the completion of Unit 1 you will be able to do the following:

1. State the names of the General Letters.
2. State one to three outline headings for each letter.
3. Match nine persons or groups with an associated description or action.
4. Match at least 25 partial teachings with their conclusions or other associated facts.
5. Identify at least 18 items as distinguishing features of a particular General Letter.

In Unit 1, as in all units of this course, you are asked to take a pre-test in order to help you learn. If you score 90 percent or more you may move directly to Unit 2. However, most people will make very low scores on the pre-test because it is on material yet to be learned. Don't let that bother you.

PRE-TEST FOR UNIT 1

A. STRUCTURE. Write on each blank the numbers of as many outline headings for each General Letter as are indicated.

James (3) _____

1 Peter (2) _____

2 Peter (2) _____
(Use ##1-7 for these three.)

1 John (3) _____

2 John (1) _____

3 John (2) _____

Jude (2) _____

1. Baptismal Sermon
2. God's Call to Life
3. Christian Practice
4. Christ's Promise and the Present
5. Christian Response to Persecution
6. Teaching and Wisdom
7. Condemnations and Warnings

8. Praise of Gaius
9. God's Command
10. Prologue: the Word
11. False Teachers
12. Christian Response
13. Living in the Light
14. Criticism of Diotrephes
15. Love and Faith

B. NARRATIVES. Write the number of each person or group on the blank before the phrase with which it is most closely associated.

____A member or a local church   1. James
____A cause of divisions   2. Peter
____Apostle and Elder   3. Paul
____Brother of James   4. John
____Spoke to God's scattered people   5. The Lady
____Lied about Elder   6. Gaius
____Sayings hard to understand   7. Diotrephes
____The Elder   8. Demetrius
____Loved the Elder's church   9. Jude
____Everyone spoke well of him   10. False teachers

C. TEACHINGS. Circle the letter of the ONE BEST answer for each.

1. 1 Peter says the prophets predicted blessings the Christian receives:
   a. Love and truth
   b. Faith and the Spirit
   c. Life and hope
   d. Energy and will
   e. a and b

2. In 1 Peter the Christian's responsibility includes ALL of the following EXCEPT:
   a. Accept the call to holy living.
   b. See that others find the Christian blessings.
   c. Obey the truth.
   d. Love fellow believers.
   e. Rid self of evil.

3. James tells Christians to be glad for problems because:
   a. They build endurance.
   b. They lead to perfection.
   c. They provide a means of achieving salvation.
   d. a and b
   e. All of the above

4. Concerning temptation, James says that:
   a. God sends all good and can't change to sending evil.
   b. God sends temptation to strengthen man.
   c. Man can prove his faith by standing firm in the face of temptation.
   d. a and c
   e. b and c

5. In 1 John the author says that the Christian is assured that he knows God:
   a. If he loves someone
   b. If he participates in the fellowship
   c. If he obeys God's commands
   d. When he avoids the darkness
   e. All of the above

6. The Christian's hope, according to 1 John, is:
   a. To become like Christ
   b. To enter heaven
   c. To love
   d. To achieve a good life
   e. a and b

7. Concerning false teachers, Jude says the Christian's actions toward others include ALL of the following EXCEPT:
   a. Showing mercy to all
   b. Saving those who doubt
   c. Rejecting those who teach falsely
   d. Hating the acts of the immoral
   e. b and d

Write the number of each partial teaching from James or Peter on the blank before the phrase with which it is most closely associated.

____Asking from selfish motives	1. Love (use twice)
____Christ's example	2. Tongue
____Delay allows more to be saved	3. Undeserved suffering
____Obeying God	4. Unbelievers
____God controls all	5. Christ's return
____In return for evil	6. No boasting
____Control	7. Praying and not receiving
____Christians should act so goodness	8. A blessing
is recognized	
____Covers many sins	

Write the number of each partial teaching from John or Jude on the blank before the phrase with which it is most closely associated.

____Deny Jesus' humanity	1. The Word
____Assurance for sinners	2. Child of God
____Punished by God	3. God is
____Love one another	4. Forgiveness through Christ
____Loves	5. New command
____Godless men	6. Part unbelievers
____Light	7. Defeat of world
____Existed from beginning	8. Distortion of truth
____Believe in Jesus as Son of God	9. False teachers

D. FEATURES. Write the names of the first three General Letters.

1. _____ 2. _____ 3. _____

Write the initial (and number, if any) of one of these three letters on the blank before each item which distinguishes that letter.

4. _____Christians to remember baptism
5. _____Saw Transfiguration
6. _____Action stressed
7. _____To all God's scattered people
8. _____How to respond in persecution
9. _____No individual interpretation of Scriptures
10. _____God gives men all they need.
11. _____Suffer for doing good.
12. _____Practice God's work.

Write the names of the last four General Letters on the blanks.

13. _____ 14. _____ 15. _____ 16. _____

Write the initial (and number, if any) of one of these letters on the blank before each item which distinguishes that letter.

17. _____Truth and love
18. _____Ungodly despise God's authority.
19. _____Love drives out fear.
20. _____Ask as God wills.
21. _____Gaius vs. Diotrephes
22. _____God is love.
23. _____Troubles predicted by apostles
24. _____No welcome for deceivers
25. _____Love one another.

Check answers and compute scores on page 9.

ANSWERS TO PRE-TEST FOR UNIT 1

A. STRUCTURE (15)   B. NARRATIVES (10)   C. TEACHINGS (25)

James: 3,6,7   5   1. c   7   9
1 Peter: 1,5   10   2. b   3   4
2 Peter: 2,4   2   3. d   5   6
1 John: 10,13,15   9   4. a   1   5
2 John: 9   1   5. c   6   2
3 John: 8,14   7   6. a   8   8
Jude: 11,12   3   7. c   2   3
                               4   4   1
                               6   1   7
                               8

D. FEATURES (25)

1. James   10. 2 Peter   19. 1 John
2. 1 Peter   11. 1 Peter   20. 2 John
3. 2 Peter   12. James   21. 3 John
4. 1 Peter   13. 1 John   22. 1 John
5. 2 Peter   14. 2 John   23. Jude
6. James   15. 3 John   24. 2 John
7. James   16. Jude   25. 1 John
8. 1 Peter   17. 2 John
9. James   18. Jude

PRE-TEST FOR UNIT 1 SCORES

Category	# Correct	% Scores	Directions
A. Structure	_____	_____	See chart below.
B. Narratives	_____	_____	# x 10 = %
C. Teachings	_____	_____	# x 4 = %
D. Features	_____	_____	# x 4 = %
Total (A+B+C+D)	_____	_____	# ÷ 3 = ____ x 4 = %

Ex.: Total # correct = 32
      32 ÷ 3 = 10 and 2 remainder, or 11
      11 x 4 = 44%

Enter ALL percent scores (category scores and total score) on Unit 1 Growth Record on page 55. If you earned 90% or more you need not study Unit 1, but should take the pre-test for Unit 2 on page 57. If you scored less than 90% (as expected), begin Unit 1 on page 11.

#	1	2	3	4	5	6	7	8	9	10	11	12	13	14	15	#
%	7	13	20	27	33	40	47	53	60	67	73	80	87	93	100	%

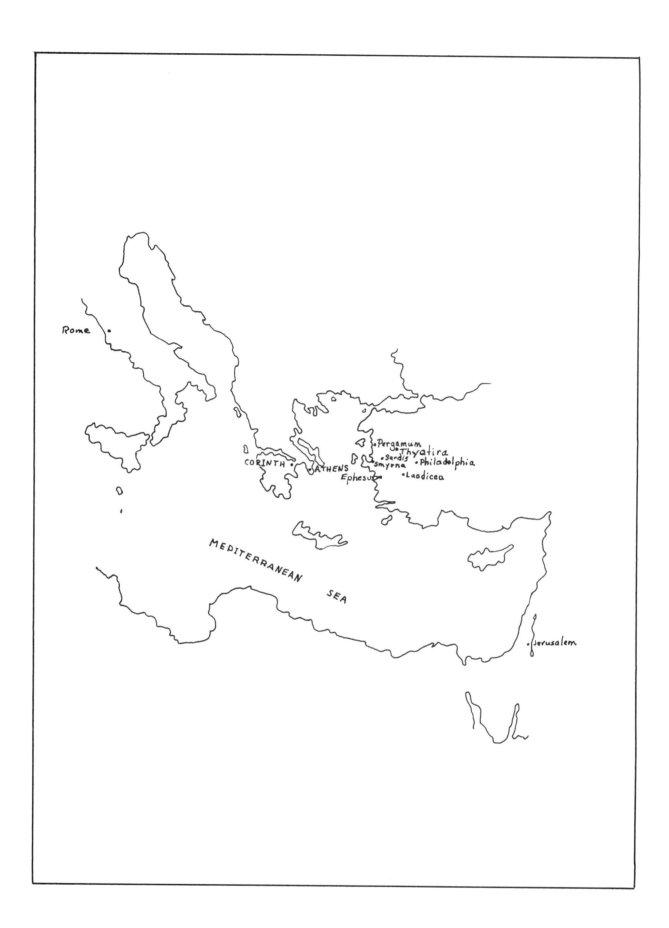

UNIT 1: THE GENERAL LETTERS

The General Letters, or Catholic Epistles, differ from the other New Testament letters in several ways. The most obvious difference is that the writer's name instead of the readers' appears in the title.

Secondly, these letters have never been attributed to Paul.

The term "catholic" means universal. These seven letters are considered as written to all Christians everywhere, although three of them mention specific readers. Note this grouping:

To All Christians:	To Specific Readers:
James	2 John (to Lady)
2 Peter	3 John (Gaius)
1 John	1 Peter (Provinces
Jude	in Asia Minor)

The General Letters are easy to remember. There are seven of them, the perfect number according to Jewish tradition. Five of the titles begin with the letter J, the first letter of "Jesus" and "Jew."

Outlines of the General Letters should be used with reserve. In the case of 1 John and James especially, if the author had a structure in mind, it is not apparent.

FROM

Non-Pauline

UNIVERSAL

7 Letters

J

I, II Peter

I, II, III John

INSTRUCTIONS

The questions which guide your reading of the New Testament have been written on divided pages, so that you do not read down a page, but turn a page after reading only one portion. This probably seems strange to you, and at first may be awkward. However, you will soon find it very helpful. After thinking of your answers to the two or three questions, you turn the page to see the answers. If the questions went straight down the page, you would have to keep turning back and forth, because you could not remember so many answers at one time.

In Unit 1, the General Letters, the questions and answers which guide the reading of James appear in the top quarter of each page, numbered in the 10's. Those which guide the reading of 1 and 2 Peter appear in the second quarter, numbered in the 20's and 30's. The questions which guide the reading of 1 John appear in the third quarter of each page and are numbered in the 40's. The questions which guide the reading of 2 and 3 John and Jude appear in the bottom quarter, numbered in the 50's, 60's, and 70's. You will read ONE BOOK at a time.

A reading assignment is given for each outline heading. To proceed:

1. Note the outline heading.
2. Read the questions about one book on one page to guide your reading.
3. Read the Bible passage assigned.
4. Reread the questions and then try to answer them from memory. (You need not write the answers unless this helps you.)
5. Look at the Bible to finish answering the questions.
6. Then and ONLY THEN turn the page to check your answers.
7. Note the drawings. They will help you remember the important points.
8. Periodically you will be referred to section charts which follow the divided pages. These section charts will add to your understanding of each book's structure (vertical), themes (horizontal), and features throughout. Fill in blanks on the charts that cover the reading you have just completed. Correct your answers and study that portion of the chart before returning to the divided page section.
9. Dividing the major section of each book is a "Just for Fun" activity. If you do not find it fun, or do not have the time, you need not do the activity. These activities involve the application of facts you have been learning and sometimes the acquisition of more information by use of references.
10. Section tests follow the section charts. After completing the divided pages and section chart for James, take the section test for James. Upon checking your answers, return to page 13 to begin the study of 1 Peter. After completing Section Test 2, turn back to page 13 to begin the study of 1 John. Using the same procedures, complete the study of 1 John and Section 4.
11. Upon completion of Section Test 4, begin Unit Test 1.
12. After checking your Unit Test answers and completing the Growth Record (growth in knowledge only), look up the references listed by any answers you missed. This will complete your mastery of basic content in the General Letters.

10 BACKGROUND OF JAMES

LITERARY TYPE: Exhortation, ethical teaching; a blend of Jewish wisdom
    literature and Greek diatribe.
AUTHOR: "James." Perhaps the Lord's brother; maybe some other James, or
    maybe pseudonymous or an interpolation.
DATE: Uncertain; probably later than Paul, but this is debated.
READERS: "The twelve tribes of the dispersion." If understood literally,
    the tract is for Jews outside Palestine, retouched for Christian use.
    If figuratively, it is for the church in general as the New Israel. A
    general tract to "all God's people."
PURPOSE: Ethical instruction for Christians; no particular circumstances.
                    (Go to top of next page.)
                ****

20 BACKGROUND OF 1 PETER

LITERARY TYPE: Sermon or homily, with letter-style opening and closing.
AUTHOR: The Apostle Peter or perhaps someone writing in his name.
DATE: Ca. A.D. 60 if by Peter; if pseudonymous, A.D. 81-96.
CIRCUMSTANCES and PURPOSE: The church was undergoing a general persecution,
    and the author wrote to remind readers of their baptism and to urge
    them to endure and hold fast. (Go to 20 on next page.)
                ****

40 BACKGROUND OF 1 JOHN

CIRCUMSTANCES and PURPOSE: The church in an unspecified region was threatened
    by schism, raising serious questions among Christians. A group that
    denied the full humanity of Jesus Christ and claimed to be sinless had
    left the fellowship. An aged authority writes to plead for adherence
    to apostolic teaching and love for fellow Christians.
LITERARY TYPE: Not really a letter, but a very personal pastoral tract.
AUTHOR: Anonymous. Traditionally the Apostle John. Scholarship attributes
    the letter to an elderly leader who shares the viewpoint of the Fourth
    Gospel.
DATE: Uncertain. Probably after the Fourth Gospel, near A.D. 100.
                    (Go to 40 on next page.)
                ****

50 BACKGROUND OF 2 JOHN

AUTHOR: "The Elder." Tradition: the Apostle John or John the Elder of
    Ephesus. Current scholarship: Uncertain, but maybe the same as the
    author of 1 John.
READER: The "dear Lady," probably a personification of a particular local
    church in Asia Minor.
LITERARY TYPE: A church letter
CIRCUMSTANCES and PURPOSE: Same false teaching that 1 John confronted. This
    pastoral letter urged the church to refuse hospitality to those who
    denied the true humanity of Jesus Christ.
DATE: Uncertain, but likely about A.D. 100.
                    (Go to 50 on next page.)

10   BACKGROUND OF JAMES

1. Literary type is:
   a. Exhortation and ethical teaching
   b. Personal letter
   c. A tract
   d. a and c

2. Readers were:
   a. Jews of the dispersion
   b. Gentiles in Asia Minor
   c. All God's people
   d. a and/or c

Check answers on previous page and proceed to next page.

****

20   BACKGROUND OF 1 PETER

1. Literary type:
   a. A sermon
   b. A personal letter to a church
   c. A letter to an individual
   d. None of the above

2. Purpose:
   a. To condemn false teaching
   b. To encourage during persecution
   c. To correct erroneous beliefs
   d. To answer questions

Check answers on previous page and proceed to 21.

****

40   BACKGROUND OF 1 JOHN

1. Circumstances:
   a. Persecution by authorities
   b. Loose living by members
   c. Group denied Jesus' humanity
   d. Insistence on keeping the Law

2. Literary type:
   a. Polemic sermon
   b. Personal letter
   c. Personal pastoral tract
   d. Formal treatise

Check answers on previous page and proceed to 41.

****

50   BACKGROUND OF 2 JOHN

1. The "Lady" was probably:
   a. Christ's bride, the universal church
   b. A strong female member
   c. The city of Rome
   d. A local church

2. Literary type:
   a. A church letter
   b. A letter to an individual
   c. A sermon

Check answers on previous page and proceed to 51.

11 OPENING: 1:1

James is the English translation of Jacob. The writer seems to indicate that he, as a patriarch of the church, is speaking to the true Israel, scattered as were the Jewish tribes in the dispersion.

(Go on to the top of the next page.)

****

21 OPENING: 1:1-2

22 A BAPTISMAL SERMON: 1:3--4:11

22A Christian Salvation. READ: 1 Peter 1:3--2:10

1. Peter describes the rich blessings the Christian receives as the prophets predicted. What are these blessings?

(Turn to 22A on the next page.)

****

41 PROLOGUE. READ: 1 John 1:1-4

What in this opening reminds one of the prologue of John's Gospel?

42 LIVING IN THE LIGHT. READ: 1 John 1:5--2:17

42A Fellowship with God: 1:5-10

1. How does John describe God?

(Turn to 42A on the next page.)

****

51 OPENING: Verses 1-3

Read: 2 John

"The Elder" refers to a church leader and "the Lady" refers to a particular church. This may be based upon the bridegroom-bride relationship used to describe Christ and his church in some of the Gospels and letters. In his address to the church, the writer introduces two qualities which his letter stresses. What are they?

(Turn to 51 on the next page.)

11   Other translations speak of the "twelve tribes" instead of "all
     God's people."

(Go on to the next page, to 12.)

****

22A

1.   New life and hope

****

42A

1.   God is light.

****

51

     Truth and love

16

12 CHRISTIAN PRACTICE. READ: James 1

1. Why are Christians told to be glad when they have problems?

****

22A Christian Salvation: 1:3--2:10

2. Having been called to holy living, the Christian will obey truth and love his fellows. Of what will he rid himself?

3. With whom does Peter identify the Christians and why?

****

42A Fellowship with God: 1:5-10

2. At the time John is writing, some men said they were without sin. What is John's answer to such a claim?

42B Fellowship with Christ: 2:1-6

1. What reassurance is given the Christian who sinned?

2. What is the Christian's assurance that he knows God?

****

52 GOD'S COMMAND: Verses 4-6

1. What is God's command to Christians?

2. What does the Elder say that love means?

12

1. Because facing problems
   results in endurance and
   perfection

****

22A

2. Of all evil

3. With the holy nation of
   Israel, because Christians
   have been chosen to be
   God's people and to proclaim the wonderful acts of God

****

42A

2. Such men deceive themselves.

42B

1. Jesus Christ is the means by
   which all sinners are forgiven.

2. That he obeys God's commandments

****

52

1. To live in truth and in love

2. Living in obedience to God's
   commands

12 CHRISTIAN PRACTICE: 1:2-27

2. What is stated in this section as the requirement for receiving what one asks in prayer?

3. Why does the writer say that temptation cannot come from God?

4. What is given as the responsibility of a man who hears the word of God?

****

22B Christian Relationships. READ: 1 Peter 2:11--3:12

1. How are Christians told to conduct themselves among believers?

2. Although Peter advised submission to state authorities and respect for the Emperor, whom are Christians told to fear?

3. Peter gives instruction concerning household relationships. Why were servants to submit even to harsh masters?

4. How are Christians to react to evil acts of others toward them?

****

42C Fellowship Within the Christian Community: 2:7-17

1. To what command do you think John is referring?

2. What does John say is true of the man who hates his brother?

****

53 THE DECEIVERS: Verses 7-11

1. How did the men whom the Elder mentions deceive others?

2. What does the Elder warn the Christians to do?

12

2. To believe that the asker will receive

3. Because God cannot be tempted by evil; every good gift comes from him and he cannot change

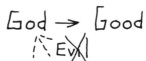

4. Putting the word into practice

****

22B

1. With conduct so good that the unbelievers have to recognize the good deeds

2. God

3. God had called them to endure undeserved suffering, following God's will and Christ's example.

4. Pay back with a blessing.

   Fill in blanks 1-6 on Section Chart 2, page 38. Check answers on page 42, study corrected chart, and continue 1 Peter on page 21.

****

42C

1. To love one another

2. He is walking in darkness.

****

53

1. By saying that Jesus Christ did not become mortal man

2. To watch themselves and stay with the true teaching of Christ

13 FAITH AND ETHICS. READ: James 2

1. What partiality is condemned?

2. What does James think about the Law for Christians?

****

22C Christian Suffering and Service. READ: 1 Peter 3:13--4:11

1. When Christians suffer for doing right and are questioned, what should they be ready to explain?

2. Of what example are Christians reminded for their undeserved suffering? What figure or type pointed to this?

3. The writer urges holy living because he thought that the end of all things was near. What does he consider most important of all and why?

****

43 DISBELIEF VS. FAITH. READ: 1 John 2:18--4:6

43A Enemies of Christ: 2:18-27
This passage refers to the last days which are described in the Gospels.

1. John speaks of many enemies of Christ. Who were they and how were they enemies?

2. Why had these enemies left the fellowship of the church, according to John?

****

53 THE DECEIVERS: Verses 7-11

3. How were the church members told to act toward a deceiver who came to their homes?

54 CONCLUSION: Verses 12-13

13

1. Special treatment because of outward appearance

2. It must be obeyed, as summarized by Jesus.

****

22C

1. Their hope

2. Christ's undeserved suffering which saved man, and Noah's "baptism," in which he was saved by water as the Christian's baptism saves him through Christ's resurrection

3. To love one another earnestly, because love covers many sins

****

43A

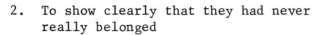

1. People who had left the Christian fellowship. They said Jesus was not the Christ.

2. To show clearly that they had never really belonged

****

53

3. They were not to welcome him or even to wish him peace.

Fill in blanks 1-6 on Section Chart 5, page 41. Check answers, page 42. Study corrected chart and turn to 60 on page 23.

13   FAITH AND ETHICS: James 2

3. How does James' statement about faith and action differ from Paul's
    as given in Romans and his other letters?

****

23   CHRISTIAN RESPONSE TO PERSECUTION. READ: 1 Peter 4:12--5:11
     In this latter part of 1 Peter, the readers were known to be under-
     going a "painful test" ("fiery trial"). Peter, who said he was an
     elder, encouraged them with a sort of pep talk.

1. Why is the Christian to expect suffering and to be glad for it?

2. How does the writer (the elder) say that resisting the Devil in spite
    of suffering will help the Christian?

24   CLOSING: 5:12-14

     Silvanus is the Latin form of Silas, Paul's associate. Mark also is
     associated with Paul and Barnabus in Acts. Babylon is the code name
     for Rome here and in the book of Revelation.

****

43B Love and Hate: 2:28--3:24

1. According to John, what is the hope that makes the Christian keep
    himself pure?

2. What does John say is the difference between the child of God and
    the child of the Devil?

3. What implication does John draw from the fact that Christ gave his
    life for man?

****

60   BACKGROUND OF 3 JOHN

AUTHOR: "The Elder," the same as 2 John
READER: Gaius, leader of a local church, probably in Asia Minor
LITERARY TYPE: A personal letter
CIRCUMSTANCES and PURPOSE: A sort of personal feud between Gaius and
    Diotrephes, competing for leadership in the church. The Elder wrote
    to encourage Gaius, to urge hospitality for itinerant Christians
    who share the truth and for Demetrius in particular.
DATE: About the same time as 2 John, probably ca. A.D. 100.

13

3. Both taught that true faith results in action, but James emphasized action, while Paul emphasized faith. (Compare James 2:18-24 with Rom. 4:1-12 and ch. 12.)

****

23

1. Christians must share Christ's suffering. Such suffering means that God's spirit is on the Christian.

2. After a while he would share God's glory and God would perfect him.

Now turn to Section Chart 2, page 38. Fill in blanks 7-10. Check answers on page 42 and study corrected chart. Then turn to page 25.

****

43B

1. That he shall become like Christ when Christ appears

2. The child of God loves what is right and loves his brother, while the child of the Devil does neither.

3. Men ought to give their lives for their brothers--not just in words, but in action.

****

60 BACKGROUND OF 3 JOHN

1. The writer, _____ wrote a letter to _____.

2. It was written because:
   a. Diotrephes needed help.
   b. Questions had been asked.
   c. Leaders were "fighting."
   d. Judaizers were causing trouble.

3. The writer encouraged ALL BUT:
   a. Gaius' work
   b. Hospitality for itinerant Christians
   c. Hospitality for Demetrius
   d. Diotrephes' work

Check previous page for answers.

24

JUST FOR FUN!!

This is an optional activity which is not tested, as are all JFF's. You may want to take a break from your study and reflect a little. James emphasizes believing one will receive the answer to prayer and action as the result of faith. This seems to have foreshadowed present theories on the creative process. Note the similarity:

Creative expectancy: Believing that what one wants will come true can often influence the person to make it come true.
Verification: The creative process is considered incomplete until disciplined effort has been applied to testing for confirmation or production.

(Turn to next page.)

****

JUST FOR FUN!!

During persecution these early Christians needed help in changing their fears to faith that the dead will live. See if you can bring hope to the lost; change hate to love; and make the dead live! Do this by changing one letter at a time, so that a new word results at each step. Maybe you can do it in fewer steps than are given here.

Ex.: sin	Try these:	LOST		HATE	Change DEAD to LIVE
1. son	1. ____		1. ____		(5 middle words)
2. soy	2. ____		2. ____		
joy	HOPE		3. ____		
			LOVE		

****

43C Criteria for Testing Prophetic Spirits: 4:1-6

1. What teaching could differentiate for the readers the man with the true Spirit from the man with the false spirit?

2. What other test could the Christian use to identify the false prophets?

****

61 OPENING: Verse 1

   READ: 3 John

62 PRAISE OF GAIUS: Verses 2-8

   Gaius was praised for his faithfulness and love. What had he done? What was he asked to do?

JUST FOR FUN!!

See if you can suggest applications of these four teachings/principles:
Pray believing/Creative expectancy
Faith in action/Verification of creative thinking

Ex.: Pray believing you will receive.
If you ask for the recovery of a sick person and believe he will be healed, you will say "When he recovers" instead of "If he pulls through." You will also find ways to hasten the recovery by sending cheery notes, providing physical or financial care, or some other way.

Think of some applications for all four, and write them down.

****

JUST FOR FUN!!

Answers can be:	LOST	HATE	DEAD
	host	late	lead
	hose	lane	lend
	HOPE	lone	lent
		LOVE	lint
			line
			LIVE

Or any legitimate combination you found!

****

43C

1. That Jesus became mortal man

2. The false prophets spoke of matters of the world and the world listened to them. They did not listen to the Christians.

Turn to Section Chart 4, page 40, and fill in blanks 1-7. Check answers, page 42, and study corrected chart. Then turn back to page 27.

****

62

He had worked for his Christian brothers even when strangers, and showed love for the Elder's church.

He was asked to help the brothers continue their trip.

14 TEACHING AND WISDOM. READ: James 3

1. What does James say is evil and that a Christian must control?

2. What difference can be observed in a man who acts upon the basis of
    heavenly wisdom and the one who is guided by worldly wisdom?

****

30 BACKGROUND OF 2 PETER

AUTHOR: According to text itself and tradition, the Apostle Peter.
    According to the vast majority of modern scholars, the letter is
    pseudonymous (written in Peter's name by a later disciple of Peter).
DATE: Mid 60's if by Peter; about A.D. 120-140 if pseudonymous.
CIRCUMSTANCES and PURPOSE: Some person or group was questioning the
    return of Christ and was living loosely; this polemic document was
    written to combat such tendencies in the church.

****

JUST FOR FUN!!

First John was written to heal a split in the church caused by false
teachers. John says false teachers can be recognized by their lack of
concern and love for their fellowmen. John stresses love as the cri-
terion for Christianity, for knowing God, and for obeying his commands.
The early church took seriously its obligation to care for the less
fortunate: orphans, widows, the elderly, the sick, those in prison.
                              (Continued on the next page.)

****

63 CRITICISM OF DIOTREPHES: Verses 9-10

1. What did the Elder find wrong with Diotrephes' actions concerning
    the Elder?

2. What had Diotrephes done wrong concerning visiting brothers?

64 PRAISE OF DEMETRIUS: Verses 11-12

    Who spoke well of Demetrius?

65 CONCLUSION: Verses 13-15

14

1. His tongue

2. Heavenly wisdom leads a man to good deeds performed in humility, and worldly wisdom to jealousy, selfishness, and disorder.

Now turn to Section Chart 1, page 37, and fill in blanks 1-6. Check answers on page 42 and continue with study on page 29.

****

30 BACKGROUND OF 2 PETER

1. If letter is pseudonymous, it was probably written:
   a. mid first century   c. early second century
   b. late first century   d. late second century

2. Letter was written because:
   a. Some persons questioned Christ's return.
   b. Some Christians were living immorally.
   c. Persecution was eliminating some church members.
   d. a and b
   e. a and c

****

JUST FOR FUN!!

Today Christians leave most of this to the state. However, there is still much for the church to do both for its members and for its neighbors, for their welfare in all its aspects.

In what ways does your church fulfill this obligation? You may want to make a list. Should it do more? In how many ways do you contribute to this work of the church? Put checks beside those ways.

****

63

1. He would not pay any attention to the Elder s letters, and told lies about him.

2. He refused to receive them, stopped those who wanted to receive them, and tried to drive them out of the church.

64 Everyone   (Now fill in blanks 1-4 on Section Chart 6, page 41.)

15 CONDEMNATIONS AND WARNINGS. READ: James 4 and 5:1-6

1. Why do many Christians not receive the things they ask God for?

                    ****

31 OPENING: 1:1-2

32 GOD'S CALL TO LIFE AND TRUTH. READ: 2 Peter 1

1. How are Christians told they can lead a godly life?

2. Peter discusses an ascending scale of eight qualities. What does
    he say an abundance of these qualities will make the Christian?

3. Instead of made-up legends, what does Peter say he can tell?

4. What does the writer say about an individual's interpretation of
    the Scriptures?

                    ****

44 LOVE AND FAITH. READ: 1 John 4--5

44A In Perfect Love: 4:7--5:3

1. After having said, "God is light," in this section, John says "God
    is love." How will God's love be made perfect in the Christian?

2. John states that perfect love will give Christians courage on
    Judgment Day. What does he say its present effect is?

                    ****

JUST FOR FUN!!

Can you find eight clues to 2 John in the February rhyme? How many clues to
3 John can you find in "Old Man Winter"?

February
28 (or 29) speaks to 30:   Old Man Winter

A valentine, a cherry tree,   He sings a song of joyful praise
A wolf in white sheepskin.   And also words of blame.
My lady will be true to me.   Watch out for ice; stay on highways;
She'll not let you in.   Say No to the reckless game.

15

1. They ask from the wrong motives, on the basis of their selfishness, not God's will.

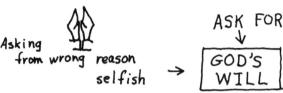

****

32

1. Through the knowledge they have been given and by divine power

2. It will make him active and effective in his knowledge of Jesus Christ.

3. About the Transfiguration, which he had seen for himself

4. No one can explain prophecy by himself because the message comes from God.

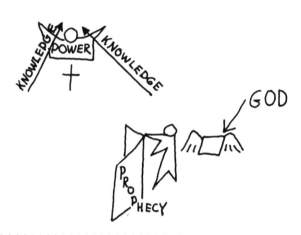

****

44A

1. As the Christian loves his brothers, God will live in him.

2. To drive out fear

****

JUST FOR FUN!!

Clues to 2 John:
Title: February is the shortest month and 2 John the shortest letter.
          Truth (or some changes) facing unbelievers:
          28 = truth; Leap Year, 29, a change; 30 = 3 persons in nothing = no God
Line 1: Love and truth (cherry tree from Washington legend)
Line 2: Deceiver
Line 3: Faith of lady reader, the church
Line 4: No hospitality to those who change the teaching (no 30 in Feb.)

Clues to 3 John:
Title: The Elder. Line 1: Praising Gaius and Demetrius (Christmas)
Line 2: Criticizing Diotrephes (bad weather)
Lines 3 and 4: Diotrephes slippery actions and reckless game--not
          allowing people to come in church (stay on highway)

15 CONDEMNATIONS AND WARNINGS: 4 and 5:1-6

2. Why is the reader not to judge a brother?

3. Why is it wrong to boast about what one would do?

****

33 THE LURE OF FALSE TEACHERS. READ: 2 Peter 2

1. Peter says that those who were denying Christ and leading immoral
    lives were making a profit out of their stories.
    a. What would happen to them?
    b. What would their many followers do?

2. Peter says that the false teachers promised freedom to others while
    they were slaves themselves. To what were they slaves, and what reason
    does Peter give for that conclusion?

3. Peter says those who accept Christ and leave him would be better off
    if they had never known him. What proverbs does he quote to describe
    such people?

****

44A In Perfect Love: 4 and 5

3. How does John say Christians show their love for God?

4. How do Christians know they love God's children?

****

70 BACKGROUND OF JUDE

CIRCUMSTANCES and PURPOSE: False teachers (probably Gnostics) in the
    churches rejected the apostolic teaching about the person of Jesus
    Christ (vs. 4) and practiced licentiousness (vss. 4, 7, 8, and 19).
    This was written to condemn them and to exhort Christians to pure
    faith and life.
LITERARY TYPE: A strong polemic manifesto, preceded by a letter opening,
    and followed by a liturgical doxology.
AUTHOR: "Jude, a servant of Jesus Christ, and the brother of James,"
    traditionally understood to be a brother of Jesus. Many scholars today
    believe the writing to be pseudonymous.
READERS: Not specified; Christians in general.
DATE: Uncertain. Guesses range from 60 if by Jesus' brother, to A.D. 140
    if pseudonymous.

15

2. Because God is the only judge

3. No man can know what the next day will bring. All is under God's control.

****

33

1. a. Sudden destruction

    b. Copy their immoral ways and speak evil of the way of truth

2. They were slaves to destructive habits because a man is a slave to anything that has defeated him.

3. "A dog goes back ..."
    "A pig that has been washed ..."

Fill in blanks 1-6 on Section Chart 3, page 39. Check answers on page 42 and continue 2 Peter on page 33.

****

44A

3. By loving their brothers

4. By loving God and obeying his commands

****

70 BACKGROUND OF JUDE

1. The situation which occasioned the letter was:
    a. A new church needing guidance
    b. Rejection of apostolic teaching
    c. Practice of immorality
    d. Disorderly worship
    e. b and c

2. The literary type is:
    a. A controversial proclamation
    b. A sermon
    c. A private letter
    d. A letter to a church
    e. Parts of two letters

Check previous page for answers.

15 CONDEMNATIONS AND WARNINGS: 4 and 5:1-6

4. What had the rich been doing that James warned them about?

****

JUST FOR FUN!!

2 Peter 2:22 mentions two proverbs. Teaching by proverbs is a Jewish literary form and one used by Jesus.

Try your hand (and your mind) at writing some proverbs on the teachings in 2 Peter. You may want to use the form of a well-known proverb.

Ex. 1: Deny your head and lose your life (2 Peter 2:16 - false teachers).

Ex. 2: He who answers the call, calls the ending. (Answering the call to a godly life allows men to enter the kingdom.)

You can probably think of better ones.

****

44B In Perfect Faith: 5:4-12

1. Who does John say can defeat the world?

2. What are the three witnesses that Jesus is the Christ?

****

71 OPENING: Verses 1-2
    READ: Jude

    How does Jude identify himself?

72 FALSE TEACHERS: Verses 3-16

1. Why was it necessary for Jude's readers to fight on for the faith?

2. Why does Jude say that God punished the Israelites after leaving Egypt, the rebelling angels, Sodom and Gomorrah, etc.?

3. How are the false teachers like those God punished?

15

4. They had kept their riches to
   themselves and had not paid
   wages to the men who had
   produced the wealth.

****

JUST FOR FUN!!

A positive teaching is given first in each case. Then a negative contrast follows in rhyme. Your task is to supply the rhyme or other word which completes
the negative teaching. The example given is from ch. 3 in which Peter explains
that the Lord's promise to return is not false, but for the purpose of wait-
ing for more men to turn from their sins.
Ex.: Turn and grow. NOT His return is too slow.
Now try these:
1. Answer the call.   NOT   Refuse and _____.
2. Saw the Son.   NOT   _____ fun.
3. Go and try.   NOT   Know; then _____.

Answers: fall, made-up, deny

****

44B

1. The one who believes that
   Jesus is the Son of God

2. The Spirit, water, and
   blood

****

72

1. Because godless men were among
   them, distorting God's message
   and rejecting Jesus Christ

2. As a warning to all

3. They reject God's authority.

JUST FOR FUN!!

Scholars say that 19 of the 25 verses of Jude appear in some form in 2 Peter.
Can you find them? (Most are in 2 Peter 2.)

16 CONCLUSION. READ: James 5:7-20

After urging patience and prayer, James gives a view of the Christian who strays which is different from that given by the writer of Hebrews. What is James' view?

****

34 CHRIST'S PROMISE AND THE PRESENT. READ: 2 Peter 3

1. How does Peter answer the argument that Christ did not keep his promise about returning?

2. What does Peter say about Paul's letters?

****

44C In Answer to Prayer: 5:13-21

1. How can the readers be sure God will hear them?

2. What are the readers told to do concerning a brother who is sinning?

****

73 THE CHRISTIANS' RESPONSE TO FALSE TEACHERS: Verses 17-23

In response to the divisions caused by these false teachers, the Christians were urged to do several things:

1. What were they to remember?

2. In what three ways were they to keep themselves safe?

3. How were they to act toward others?

74 CONCLUSION: PRAYER OF PRAISE (Doxology): Verses 24-25

16

Fellow Christians can bring back
those who have turned away from
the truth.

Fill in blanks 7-9 on Section Chart 1, page 37. Check answers on page 42,
study chart, and then take Section Test 1 on page 43.

****

34

1. Time means little to God.
    He is waiting for men to
    turn from their sins.

2. Ignorant and unstable
    people were explaining some
    of the difficult parts
    falsely.

Turn to page 39 and complete Section Chart 3, blanks 7 and 8. Check answers on
page 42 and study corrected chart. Then take Section Test 2 on page 45.

****

44C

1. By asking according to his will

2. To pray for him if it was not a
    sin that leads to death. (The "sin
    that leads to death" may refer to
    2:19, separating oneself from the
    church, or to 2:22, false under-
    standing of Jesus Christ.)

Fill in blanks 8-11, Section Chart 4, on page 40. Check answers, page 42,
and then take Section Test 3 on page 47.

****

73

1. The predictions of the apostles

2. Keep building themselves in the
    faith; pray in the power of the
    Spirit; keep themselves in the
    love of God

3. To show mercy to all, to save those
    who have doubts, but to hate the acts
    of the immoral

Now complete Sect. Chart 7, p. 42, and then take Sect. Test 4, p. 49.

36

SECTION CHART 1: JAMES

OPENING 1:1

James

The (1) _____ True Israel

CHRISTIAN PRACTICE Ch. 1

GLAD FOR 2.
PRAY BELIEVING
EVERY GOOD GIFT
3.
THE WORD

FAITH AND ETHICS Ch. 2

Don't judge by appearances

OBEY LAW

Faith without (4) _____ is dead

TEACHING AND WISDOM Ch. 3

Control your (5) _____

Heavenly wisdom:

Good (6) _____, in humility

Worldly wisdom:

Selfishness, disorder

CONDEMNATIONS AND WARNINGS 4 and 5:1-6

Selfish prayer not (7) _____

Gimme! Gimme!

DON'T

Judge or (8) ____

Rich Men:

Watch Out!

CONCLUSION 5:7-20

Have Patience!

Pray!

(9) _____ the brother who strayed!

Check answers on page 42 and study the corrected chart.

SECTION CHART 2: FIRST PETER

SALVATION 1:1--2:10

Blessings:

Predicted by
the prophets

(1) _____

Responsibilities

Obey truth
(2) _____
believers
Get rid of
(3) _____

B
A
P
T
I

_____ Christians: The New Holy Nation of Israel _____

CHRISTIAN RELATIONSHIPS 2:11--3:12

Make
(4) _____
recognize
goodness

Submit to
(5) _____

W
i
t
h

(6) _____
God

Household
Servants: submit

S
M
A
L
S
E

_____ Pay back evil with a blessing. _____

SUFFERING   3:13--4:11

Suffer for

(7) _____

Ex.

HOPE

HAPPINESS

Suffering

Love covers

(8) _____

R
M
O
N

RESPONSE TO PERSECUTION 4:12--5:14

Be glad to share
suffering
with (9) _____

A word from the
(10) _____

Resist the Devil

Suffer for a while

Then glory and
perfection

P
E
P

T
A
L
K

Check answers page 42, and study corrected chart.

OPENING 1:1-2

GOD'S CALL TO LIFE Ch. 1

God

gives

all

men need

to live a

godly

life.

(1)

Brotherly
love

Godliness

Endurance

Knowledge

Goodness

Faith

These virtues
make Christians effective.

Eyewitness:

No myth, saw

(2) _____

Scriptures by
Holy Spirit

(3) _____
by individuals

LURE OF FALSE TEACHERS   Ch. 2

Denial of Jesus
and
(4) _____
ways

Sudden

(5) _____

God's past judgment

NOAH

False teachers
promise (6) _____
but
are slaves to habits

Proverbs

CHRIST'S PROMISE AND THE PRESENT   Ch. 3

When?

1 day = 1,000 years

Delay so more

(7) _____

THE DAY
of the
LORD

Will come
as a thief at
night

Paul:

Use delay as
opportunity

Paul's hard sayings

(8) _____

by the ignorant

Be on guard against error! Grow in the Lord!

Check answers on page 42, and study corrected chart.

SECTION CHART 4: FIRST JOHN

PROLOGUE 1:1-4
Word of Life - From the Beginning

LIVING IN THE LIGHT 1:5--2:17
Means fellowship with:

God 1:5-10	Christ 2:1-6	Christians 2:7-17

God is:

(1) _____

(2) _____
for sinners

God's command:

(3) _____

DISBELIEF VS. FAITH 2:18--4:6

Enemies of Christ	Love and Hate	Testing False Spirits

Ex-Christians:
  Jesus NOT the
    Christ

They never really
(4) _____ to
  the fellowship

Child of God:
(5) _____

Child of
Devil:
(6) _____

Christian HOPE:
To become like

They teach:
  Jesus Christ was not
(7) _____

They speak of
  worldly matters.

°NUDES°

LOVE AND FAITH 4:7--5:21

Perfect Love	Perfect Faith	Answer to Prayer

God is
(8) _____

Love drives out
(9) _____

Believe in Jesus
as Son of God
      and
(10) _____
    the world

Ask as God

(11) _____

Check answers on page 42 and study corrected chart.

SECTION CHART 5: SECOND JOHN

OPENING 1-3

From the (1) _____ to the Lady

Truth and (2) _____

GOD'S (3) _____ 4-6

THE WORD
TRUTH

Live in
AND

LOVE

DECEIVERS 7-17

They say:
Jesus Christ
did not
become (4) _____
man

So watch out!

Christians must
(5) _____ the
teaching of Christ

No (6) _____ for them!

CONCLUSION 12-13

Check answers on page 42 and study corrected chart.

SECTION CHART 6: THIRD JOHN

OPENING 1
From the Elder to Gaius

PRAISE OF GAIUS 2-8

Faithful

To the
(1) _____

Love for Elder's church

In working for

(2) _____

CRITICISM OF DIOTREPHES 9-10

Elder to
Diotrephes

(3) _____
about Elder

Visiting brothers:

He tried to

(4) _____ them

_____

STOP

PRAISE OF DEMETRIUS 11-12

Everyone speaks well of him.

CONCLUSION 13-15

Check answers, page 42, study corrected chart, then turn to page 29.

SECTION CHART 7: JUDE

OPENING 1-2

From: The Servant of Jesus Christ, the (1) _____ of James

FALSE TEACHERS 3-16

Christians (2) _____
  for the faith.

God (3) _____
  unbelievers in the past

1+2 = 5

The immoral reject
  Jesus Christ

The present ungodly
  despise God's
  (4) _____

THE CHRISTIANS' (5) _____ 17-23

Troubles predicted
  by (6) _____

Keep selves in (7) _____
  and love. Pray, show mercy.

CONCLUSION 24-25

****

ANSWERS TO SECTION CHARTS

James
1. Scattered
2. Problems
3. Practice
4. Activities
5. Tongue
6. Deeds
7. Answered
8. Boast
9. Bring back

1 Peter
1. Life
2. Love
3. Evil
4. Unbelievers
5. Authorities (state)
6. Fear
7. Doing good
8. Many sins
9. Christ
10. Elder

2 Peter
1. Love
2. Transfiguration
3. Interpretation
4. Immoral
5. Destruction
6. Freedom
7. Will be saved
8. Misunderstood

1 John
1. Light
2. Forgiveness
3. Love one another
4. Belonged
5. Love
6. Hates
7. Mortal man
8. Love
9. Fear
10. Defeat
11. Wills

2 John
1. Elder
2. Love
3. Command
4. Mortal
5. Stay with
   (keep)
6. Welcome

3 John
1. Truth
2. Brothers
3. Lied
4. Drive from
   the church

Jude
1. Brother
2. Fight on
3. Punished
4. Authority
5. Response
6. Apostles
7. Faith

SECTION TEST 1:   JAMES

A.   STRUCTURE.   Fill in the blanks in the following outline of James.

    Opening
  I.   Christian (1) _____
 II.   (2) _____ and _____
III.   Teaching and (3) _____
 IV.   (4) _____ and _____
    Conclusion

C.   TEACHINGS.   Circle the letter of the ONE BEST answer.

1.   James told the readers to ask God for wisdom, and to receive it,
   a.   They should pray with others.
   b.   They should do good to others.
   c.   They should believe they will receive it.
   d.   They must earn it.
   e.   b and c

2.   In order to explain that God never tempts man, James says:
   a.   "Every good gift comes down from God."
   b.   "God does not change."
   c.   "Consider yourself fortunate when trials come your way."
   d.   "... mercy triumphs over judgment."
   e.   a and b

3.   ALL of the following situations make the Law judge a Christian
   EXCEPT when:
   a.   He ignores Christ's summary of the Law by showing partiality.
   b.   He breaks one part of it.
   c.   He makes judgments based on evil motives.
   d.   He ignores the little laws and substitutes general love.
   e.   He treats a rich person better than a poor one.

4.   Some Christians did not receive what they asked in prayer even though
   they believed because:
   a.   Their faith was weak.
   b.   They asked for their own pleasures.
   c.   They had everything they needed.
   d.   They were sinners.
   e.   a and b

5.   Speaking against a brother was said to be wrong for ALL the following
   reasons EXCEPT:
   a.   The person was speaking against the Law.
   b.   The person was not respecting his brother's privacy.
   c.   The person was not obeying the Law.
   d.   The person was judging the Law.
   e.   God is the only lawgiver and judge.

6. Rich men were described in ALL the following ways EXCEPT:
   a. Piling up riches
   b. Creating wealth
   c. Not paying wages to their workers
   d. Filling their own lives with luxury and pleasure
   e. Having condemned and murdered the innocent man

7. Paul says that true faith results in action. James:
   a. Says the same
   b. Says that action is more important than faith
   c. Stresses action more than faith
   d. Stresses faith more than action
   e. a and c

Write the number of the partial teaching on the blank of the phrase with which it is most closely associated. Use each number ONCE.

____ Judging by appearances	1. Problems are good
____ Selfishness and disorder	2. Hear the word
____ Develop endurance	3. Evil motives
____ God controls all	4. No boasting
____ Believers can help	5. The tongue
____ Practice	6. Wordly wisdom
____ Spread of evil	7. Fallen Christian

D.   FEATURES.   Draw a circle around the number of seven of the following items which distinguish James from the basic or prison letters.

1. Author gives his name as James.
2. Anonymous
3. To the twelve tribes of the dispersion
4. Action is stressed
5. Saved through faith by grace
6. Love is patient and kind
7. Christ is in first place
8. To all God's people
9. Unity of the body
10. "Every good gift comes down from God."
11. "Keep on working to complete your salvation."
12. "You must believe when you pray, and not doubt at all."
13. Practicing word is responsibility of those who hear it.
14. "Fill your minds with those things ..."

Check answers on page 50 and compute scores on page 51. Then turn to page 13 to begin 1 Peter.

SECTION TEST 2:   1 and 2 PETER

A.   STRUCTURE.   Fill in the blanks of the following outlines.

<u>1 Peter</u>   <u>2 Peter</u>

   Opening   I. God's (3) _____
I. A (1) _____ Sermon   II. The Lure of False Teachers
II. Christian (2) _____   III. Christ's (4)_____

   _____

B.   NARRATIVES.   Write the number of the name of the person on the blank
                before the word or phrase with which it is most closely
                associated.

____ Sometimes hard to understand   1. Peter (in 1 Peter)
____ Saw Transfiguration   2. Peter (in 2 Peter)
____ Elder   3. Paul

C.   TEACHINGS.   Circle the letter of the ONE BEST answer in 1 Peter.

1. According to Peter, the Christian's blessings of life and hope have:
    a. Always been given to all men
    b. Been predicted by the prophets
    c. Still to be won
    d. Never been known
    e. c and d

2. The writer says that God's call to Christians to be holy and to proclaim
    the gospel:
    a. Is not understood by the church
    b. Is their way of earning salvation
    c. Makes them better persons than unbelievers
    d. Makes Christians the people of God, the New Israel
    e. b and d

3. Peter advised Christians who experienced evil acts against them to:
    a. Report them to the authorities
    b. Stand up for their rights
    c. Pay back with a blessing
    d. Be glad men are cruel so they can display goodness
    e. Accept the suffering stoically

4. Christians can be glad for their sufferings for ALL of the following
    reasons EXCEPT:
    a. Christ's undeserved suffering has saved them.
    b. They are sharing Christ's suffering.
    c. It means God's Spirit has come down on them.
    d. It is evidence of their hope.
    e. The Christian's suffering removes his sins.

5. The individual Christian should keep his faith and resist the Devil because:
   a. He will be perfected by God eventually.
   b. He will then share God's glory.
   c. He will suffer.
   d. Others will believe when they see his faith.
   e. a and b

Circle the ONE BEST answer from 2 Peter.

6. Peter says that God's call to a perfect life can be met because:
   a. Man is capable of attaining it.
   b. All people received it upon Christ's resurrection.
   c. God gives all that is needed for it.
   d. The prophets predicted it.
   e. All of the above

7. ALL of the following were true of the false teachers EXCEPT:
   a. Their teachings led to destruction.
   b. They denied Jesus Christ.
   c. They considered pleasure to be physical indulgence.
   d. They were greedy.
   e. They found freedom in life.

8. Peter says that the Christians who leave Christ to follow false teachers:
   a. Can correct their teachings
   b. Are worse for having known Christ and then left him
   c. Should be brought back to repentance
   d. Are like Lot
   e. c and d

Write the number of each partial teaching on the blank before the ONE phrase with which it is most closely associated.

_____ Their hope in suffering   1. Noah's flood
_____ Fellow believers   2. Individual interpretation of
_____ To win more men   Scriptures
_____ No one can explain by himself. 3. Christians to love
_____ No one knows.   4. Christians to explain
_____ Christian's baptism   5. Time of Christ's return
_____ A fellow Christian   6. A washed pig
                                        7. Delayed return

D. FEATURES. Write 1 P or 2 P in the blank before each of three phrases which distinguishes one of these letters.
1. ____ Warmly personal letter   4. ____ Stresses action
2. ____ Blessings and responsibilities 5. ____ Christ as priest
3. ____ Stresses hope   6. ____ To God 1,000 years like a day

Check answers on page 50 and compute scores on page 51.

SECTION TEST 3: 1 JOHN

A. STRUCTURE. Fill in the blanks of the following outline of 1 John.

      Prologue
  I. Living (1) _____
 II. (2) _____ vs. _____
III. (3) _____ and _____

C. TEACHINGS. Circle the ONE BEST answer for each statement.

1. The Word of life:
    a. Was created with the world
    b. Existed from the beginning
    c. Came into being when Jesus was resurrected
    d. Came to Jesus at his baptism
    e. Had already been revealed to man

2. A Christian lives in the light through his fellowship with:
    a. God and Christ
    b. Christ and the Christian community
    c. God and the world
    d. a and b
    e. All of the above

3. John emphasized God as:
    a. Light
    b. Love
    c. Judge
    d. a and b
    e. All of the above

4. John says that one who hates his brother:
    a. Walks in darkness
    b. Is a child of the Devil
    c. Does not know God
    d. Is a sinner
    e. All of the above

5. John says ALL of the following about real love EXCEPT:
    a. It results in action.
    b. It means that one obeys God's commands.
    c. It means that one loves the world.
    d. It drives out fear.
    e. Christians love God by loving men.

6. ALL of the following identify false teachers EXCEPT:
    a. The teaching that Jesus Christ did not become mortal man
    b. Speaking about matters of material concern to the world
    c. Gaining the world's attention
    d. Working hard
    e. Not listening to Christian teachings

7. The three witnesses that Jesus is the Christ are given as:
   a. Spirit, water, blood
   b. Spirit, prophets, Scriptures
   c. Scriptures, creation, Spirit
   d. Scriptures, angels, apostles
   e. God the Father, the Holy Spirit, the church of God

8. Christians could be sure God would answer their prayers when:
   a. They prayed according to God's will.
   b. They asked help for a brother who was sinning.
   c. They prayed for a Christian who denied Christ.
   d. a and b
   e. All of the above

Write the number of each partial teaching on the blank before the ONE phrase
with which it is most closely associated. (One phrase will have two numbers.)

_____ Sin		1. Reassurance for sinners
_____ Obedience to God's commands		2. Assurance of knowing God
_____ Worldly matters		3. Christian hope
_____ Jesus Christ: means of		4. Assurance of loving others
forgiveness		5. Believe Jesus is Son of God
_____ Defeat the world.		6. All men
_____ Be like Christ.		7. False teachers

D. FEATURES. Circle the numbers of seven items which distinguish 1 John
                from James and 1 and 2 Peter.
 1. To all God's people
 2. Do not doubt when you pray.
 3. To a church threatened by schism
 4. Hear the word? Then practice it.
 5. God is light.
 6. God is love.
 7. From the Elder
 8. Paul's sayings are sometimes hard to understand.
 9. Pray according to God's will.
10. Saw the Transfiguration
11. Love drives out fear.
12. Love covers many sins.
13. Child of God loves.
14. Give lives for others in action.

Check answers on page 50 and compute scores on page 51.

#	1	2	3	4	5	6		#
%	17	33	50	67	83	100		%

#	1	2	3	4	5	6	7	#
%	14	29	43	57	71	86	100	%

SECTION TEST 4: 2 and 3 JOHN and JUDE

A. STRUCTURE. Fill in the blanks of these outlines.

      2 John   3 John

  I. God's (1) _____   I. (3) _____

 II. The (2) _____   II. (4) _____

       Jude   III. (5) _____

  I. (6) _____

 II. The (7) _____

B. NARRATIVES. Write the number of the person or group on the blank before
               the ONE phrase with which it is most closely associated.

____ Faithful and helped brothers   1. Elder
____ Tradition: John the apostle   2. Lady
      or John of Ephesus   3. Deceivers
____ All spoke well of him   4. Gaius
____ To be refused hospitality   5. Diotrephes
____ Brother of James   6. Demetrius
____ May be personification of a   7. Jude
      particular church
____ Ignored Elder's advice

D. FEATURES. Write 2J, 3J, or Jd in the blank before each item which is a
               distinguishing feature of 2 John, 3 John, or Jude.

1. ____ Praise and criticism
2. ____ Ungodly despise God's authority
3. ____ Stresses love and truth
4. ____ God punished unbelievers in the past.
5. ____ Denial of Jesus' humanity by some
6. ____ Troubles predicted by apostles

Check answers on page 50 and compute scores below. Then enter ALL percent scores
on page 55, and take Unit Test 1, page 52.

Category	# Correct	% Score	Directions
A. Structure	_____	_____	See chart, p. 48, for 7#.
B. Narratives	_____	_____	See chart, p. 48, for 7#.
D. Features	_____	_____	See chart, p. 48, for 6#.
Total (A+B+D)	_____	_____	# x 5 = %

ANSWERS TO SECTION TESTS FOR UNIT 1

Test 1

A. STRUCTURE (4)	C. TEACHINGS (14)		D. FEATURES (7)
1. Practice	1. c	3	1
2. Faith and Ethics	2. e	6	3
3. Wisdom	3. d	1	4
4. Condemnations and	4. e	4	7
Warnings	5. b	7	10
	6. b	2	12
	7. e	5	13

Test 2

A. STRUCTURE (4)	B. NARRATIVES (3)	C. TEACHINGS (15)		D. FEATURES (3)
1. Baptismal	3	1. b	4	2. 1 P
2. Response to	2	2. d	3	3. 1 P
Persecution	1	3. c	7	6. 2 P
3. Call to Life		4. e	2	
and Truth		5. e	5	
4. Promise and		6. c	1	
the Present		7. e	6	
		8. b		

Test 3

A. STRUCTURE (3)	C. TEACHINGS (15)		D. FEATURES (7)
1. In the Light	1. b	6	3
2. Disbelief vs. Faith	2. d	2,4	5
3. Love and Faith	3. d	7	6
	4. e	1	9
	5. c	5	11
	6. d	3	13
	7. a		14
	8. d		

Test 4

A. STRUCTURE (7)	B. NARRATIVES (7)	D. FEATURES (6)
1. Command	4	1. 3 J
2. Deceivers	1	2. Jd
3. Praise of Gaius	6	3. 2 J
4. Criticism of Diotrephes	3	4. Jd
5. Praise of Demetrius	7	5. 2 J
6. False Teachers	2	6. Jd
7. Christians' Response	5	

SECTION TEST 1 SCORES

Category	# Correct	% Score	Directions
A. Structure	_____	_____	# x 25 = %
C. Teachings	_____	_____	See chart below for 14 #.
D. Features	_____	_____	See chart for 7 #, p. 48.
Total (A+C+D)	_____	_____	# x 4 = %

Enter ALL percent scores on Unit Growth Record, page 55. After reviewing items missed, begin the study of 1 Peter on page 13.

SECTION TEST 2 SCORES

Category	# Correct	% Score	Directions
A. Structure	_____	_____	# x 25 = %
B. Narratives	_____	_____	# x 33 = ___ + 1 = %
C. Teachings	_____	_____	See chart below for 15 #.
D. Features	_____	_____	# x 33 = ___ + 1 = %
Total (A+B+C+D)	_____	_____	# x 4 = %

Enter ALL percent scores on Unit Growth Record, page 55. After reviewing items missed, begin the study of 1 John on page 13.

SECTION TEST 3 SCORES

Category	# Correct	% Score	Directions
A. Structure	_____	_____	# x 33 = ___ + 1 = %
C. Teachings	_____	_____	See chart for 15 #.
D. Features	_____	_____	See chart for 7 #.
Total (A+C+D)	_____	_____	# x 4 = %

Enter ALL percent scores on Unit Growth Record, page 55. After reviewing items missed, begin the study of 2 John on page 13.

#	1	2	3	4	5	6	7	8	9	10	11	12	13	14	#
%	7	14	21	28	36	43	50	57	64	71	79	86	93	100	%

#	1	2	3	4	5	6	7	8	9	10	11	12	13	14	15	#
%	7	13	20	27	33	40	47	53	60	67	73	80	87	93	100	%

UNIT TEST 1:   GENERAL LETTERS

A.   STRUCTURE.   Fill in the blanks on these outlines.

		James				1 John
1.	I.	Christian _____	8.			_____
	II.	Faith and Ethics		I.	Living in the Light	
2.	III.	Teaching and _____	9.	II.	_____ vs. _____	
3.	IV.	_____	10.	III.	_____ and _____	

		1 Peter				2 John
4.	I.	_____ Sermon	11.	I.	_____	
5.	II.	Christian _____		II.	The Deceivers	
		to _____				

		2 Peter				3 John
6.	I.	God's _____	12.	I.	_____	
	II.	The Lure of False Teachers	13.	II.	_____	
7.	III.	Christ's _____		III.	Praise of Demetrius	
		and _____				Jude
			14.	I.	_____	
			15.	II.	Christians' _____	

B.   NARRATIVES.   Write the number of each person or group on the blank
     before the phrase with which it is most closely associated.   Use each
     number ONCE unless marked TWICE.   ONE phrase will have TWO numbers
     before it.

_____ Saw Transfiguration	1.	Paul
_____ Brother of James	2.	Peter (use twice)
_____ Perhaps a local church	3.	John
_____ Well-spoken of by all	4.	The Lady
_____ Elder	5.	Gaius
_____ Sayings hard to understand	6.	Diotrephes
_____ Helped visitors	7.	Demetrius
_____ Denial of Christ	8.	Jude
_____ Tried to drive Christians	9.	The false teachers
out of church		

C.   TEACHINGS.   Circle the letter of the ONE BEST answer.

1.   1 John says that love for God means:
     a. Appreciating the brothers
     b. Obeying God's commands
     c. Living
     d. Action
     e. a and d

2. Warning Christians of the source of its power as hell, James tells them to:
   a. Resist the persecution
   b. Avoid the immoral life
   c. Give up their worship of false spirits
   d. Control their tongues
   e. b and e

3. Peter says that loving one another is most important because:
   a. Love covers many sins.
   b. God is love.
   c. Love is the new commandment.
   d. All men need love.
   e. a and b

4. In 1 Peter the Christians' undeserved suffering is said to be:
   a. Like that of their example, Christ
   b. A wrong which will be righted
   c. The result of their disobedience
   d. A source of hope and happiness
   e. a and d

5. In discussing Christian salvation, 1 Peter speaks at length of:
   a. Christ's superiority to the other spirits
   b. The sacrifice of many believers
   c. The destruction facing unbelievers
   d. Life in heaven with the Lord
   e. Blessings and responsibilities

6. 1 Peter advises Christians of ALL their relationships as follows EXCEPT:
   a. With fellow believers: Work to prevent suffering.
   b. With unbelievers: Make them recognize goodness.
   c. With God: Fear him
   d. Within households: Servants, submit even to harsh masters.
   e. With state authorities: Submit to them.

7. 2 Peter states ALL of the following about false teachers EXCEPT:
   a. They are slaves to habits.
   b. They deny Jesus.
   c. They live immorally.
   d. They ignore the Christians.
   e. They will be destroyed.

8. In 2 Peter, ALL of the following are said about Christ's return EXCEPT:
   a. It will come as a thief in the night.
   b. Study the Scriptures to learn the time of the return.
   c. To God a day is as 1,000 years.
   d. Be on guard against error.
   e. Use delay as opportunity.

Write the number of each partial teaching from <u>James</u> and <u>Peter</u> on the blank before the ONE phrase with which it is most closely associated.

_____ Sharing with Christ	1.	Unanswered prayer
_____ God gives all that is needed	2.	God, the only judge
_____ Speaking against a brother	3.	No boasting
_____ Obey the truth and love believers	4.	Experience evil acts
_____ Asking selfishly	5.	Christian responsibility
_____ More will be saved	6.	God's call to a perfect life
_____ God controls all	7.	False teachers
_____ Promise freedom	8.	Be glad for suffering
_____ Pay back with a blessing	9.	Return delayed

Write the number of each partial teaching from <u>John</u> and <u>Jude</u> on the blank before the ONE phrase with which it is most closely associated.

_____ Existed from the beginning	1.	God's command (use twice)
_____ Love one another	2.	The Word
_____ Hate acts of the immoral	3.	False teachers
_____ With God, Christ, Christian	4.	God
community	5.	Living in the light
_____ Jesus did not become mortal	6.	One who hates
_____ Live in truth and love	7.	As show mercy to all
_____ Light		
_____ Walks in darkness		

D. FEATURES. Write the names of the first three General Letters on these blanks.

1. _____ 2. _____ 3. _____

Now write the initial of each (and number, if any) on the blank before each item to identify it as a distinguishing feature.

4. _____ To all God's people	9.	_____	Practice the word
5. _____ Stresses action	10.	_____	No interpretation of Scripture by individual
6. _____ Reminder of baptism during persecution	11.	_____	Pray believing that you will receive
7. _____ Saw Transfiguration	12.	_____	The New Israel
8. _____ Life and hope			

Write the names of the last four General Letters on the first four blanks. Then write the initial (and number, if any) before each item to identify it as a distinguishing feature of one of the last four General Letters.

1. _____ 2. _____ 3. _____ 4. _____			
5. _____ The Elder and the Lady	9.	_____	The Word at creation
6. _____ Split on Jesus' humanity	10.	_____	Love drives out fear
7. _____ The Elder to Gaius	11.	_____	Brother of James
8. _____ Ungodly despise God's authority	12.	_____	Truth and Love
	13.	_____	God is love

Check answers on page 56 and compute scores on page 55.

UNIT TEST 1 SCORES

Category	# Correct	% Score	Directions
A. Structure	_____	_____	See chart below for 15 #.
B. Narratives	_____	_____	# x 10 = %
C. Teachings	_____	_____	# x 4 = %
D. Features	_____	_____	# x 4 = %
Total (A+B+C+D)	_____	_____	# ÷ 3 = ____ x 4 = %

Sample total score computation:
   # correct = 71 ÷ 3 = 23 remainder 2 or 24 x 4 = 96%
   # correct = 64 ÷ 3 = 21 remainder 1 or 21 x 4 = 84%

#	1	2	3	4	5	6	7	8	9	10	11	12	13	14	15	#
%	7	13	20	27	33	40	47	53	60	67	73	80	87	93	100	%

Enter ALL percent scores on the Unit Growth Record below. Then subtract your pre-test score from your unit test score in each category to see your growth in knowledge of the General Letters.

UNIT 1 GROWTH RECORD

Category	Pre-test	Sect. 1	Sect. 2	Sect. 3	Sect. 4	Unit	Growth
A. Structure	%	%	%	%	%	%	%
B. Narratives		xxxx		xxxx			
C. Teachings					xxxx		
D. Features							
Total							

Be sure to look up references for any items missed before starting Unit 2.

ANSWERS TO UNIT TEST 1

A. STRUCTURE (15). (See headings and charts for errors.)

1. Practice
2. Wisdom
3. Condemnations and
     Warnings
4. Baptismal
5. Response to
     Persecution (Pep Talk)
6. Call to Life
7. Promise and
     the Present
8. Prologue: The Word

9. Disbelief vs. Faith
10. Love and Faith
11. God's Command
12. Praise of Gaius
13. Criticism of Diotrephes
14. False Teachers
15. Response

B. NARRATIVES (10)

    2   (2 P 1:17-18)
    8   (Jd)
    4   (2 J 1)
    7   (3 J 12)
2, 3   (2 J 1; 1 P 5:1)
    1   (2 P 3:16)
    5   (3 J 5, 6)
    9   (1 J 2:22; 2 J 7)
    6   (3 J 10)

C. TEACHINGS (25)

1. b (1 J 5:3)   8 (1 P 4:13)   2 (1 J 1:1)
2. d (Jas 3:8-10)   6 (2 P 1:3)   1 (1 J 3:11)
3. a (1 P 4:8)   2 (Jas 4:11-12)   7 (Jd 23)
4. e (1 P 2:20-21)   5 (1 P 1:22)   5 (1 J 1:3-7)
5. e (1 P 1:4--   1 (Jas 4:3)   3 (1 J 4:2-3)
         2:10)   9 (2 P 3:9)   1 (2 J 4, 5)
6. a (1 P 2:12-18)   3 (Jas 4:13-16)   4 (1 J 1:5)
7. d (2 P 2:1-3,   7 (2 P 2:19)   6 (1 J 2:11)
         19)   4 (1 P 3:9)
8. b (2 P 3:8-10,
     15, 17)

D. FEATURES (25)

1. James
2. 1 Peter
3. 2 Peter
4. James (1:1)
5. James (2:14-26)
6. 1 Peter (p. 13)
7. 2 Peter (1:17-18)
8. 1 Peter (1:3)
9. James (1:22-23)
10. 2 Peter (1:20-21)
11. James (1:6)
12. 1 Peter (2:9)

1. 1 John
2. 2 John
3. 3 John
4. Jude
5. 2 John (1)
6. 1 John (p. 13)
7. 3 John (1)
8. Jude (8)
9. 1 John (1:1)
10. 1 John (4:18)
11. Jude (1)
12. 2 John (1, 4-5)
13. 1 John (4:8)

UNIT 2: REVELATION
OBJECTIVES [APOCALYPSE] [REVELATION]

After completing the study of Unit 2 you will be able to do the following:

1. State the major headings of Revelation.
2. State in order of appearance in Revelation the three series of plagues.
3. State at least six series of visions.
4. Identify at least nine characters by their actions, descriptions, or accounts.
5. Identify at least five groups of persons by their actions, characteristics, or other associations.
6. Identify at least four places by their descriptions or the actions which are reported there.
7. State the name of the writer.
8. Identify the writer's situation.
9. Identify the meanings of at least 15 symbols used in Revelation.
10. Identify at least four kinds of features which distinguish Revelation.

PRE-TEST FOR UNIT 2

A. STRUCTURE. Circle the letter of the ONE BEST answer.

1. The major headings for Revelation are:
    a. Heaven; The Dragon
    b. Letters; Apocalypse
    c. The Churches; Christ
    d. Letters; Dragon
    e. Apocalypse; The Fall of Babylon

2. The three series of plagues are recorded in this order:
    a. Bowls, seals, trumpets
    b. Seals, trumpets, lamps
    c. Seals, trumpets, bowls
    d. Trumpets, bowls, lamps
    e. Lamps, trumpets, bowls

3. Other major visions are:
    a. Christ, Throne, Dragon
    b. Babylon, Beasts, Woman
    c. Christ, Satan, New Jerusalem
    d. b and c
    e. All of above

Circle the numbers of TWO large important subdivisions of Revelation.

1. Christ, Heaven, and Hell
2. Heaven, Earth, and God's people
3. The Return of Christ
4. The Lion, Lamb, and Eagle

B. NARRATIVES. Write the number of EACH of the following persons or animals on the blank before the ONE term with which it is most closely associated.

_____ Jesus Christ		1.	Worthy one
_____ Give authority to beast		2.	John
_____ False prophet		3.	Woman's son
_____ To rule all nations with rod		4.	Rider of white horse
_____ 666		5.	Bride of lamb
_____ Announcer of more horrors		6.	Michael
_____ Opened seals		7.	Dragon
_____ War in heaven		8.	Beast of sea
_____ New Jerusalem		9.	Beast of earth
_____ Ate scroll		10.	Eagle

Write the number of EACH place on the blank before the term with which it is most closely associated.

_____ Church addressee of a letter	1.	Patmos
_____ Seven hills	2.	Philadelphia
_____ Battle at end of world	3.	Asia
_____ Province of seven churches	4.	Rome
_____ Island of imprisonment	5.	Armageddon

Write the number of each group of persons on the blank before the term which most closely identifies that group.

_____ 144,000	1.	Seven churches
_____ Fall of Babylon	2.	Martyrs
_____ Victories to be rewarded	3.	Mourners
_____ Came through persecution	4.	First to be redeemed
_____ To rule with Christ	5.	Great crowd

C. FEATURES. Circle the ONE BEST answer.

1. Authorship of Revelation is
    a. Anonymous
    b. By Paul
    c. Without human intermediary
    d. By John
    e. By the brother of Jesus

2. Revelation was written from Patmos because:
    a. An important church was there.
    b. The writer was in prison there.
    c. An Essene library was there.
    d. It was the center of persecution then.
    e. b and d

3. Seven, a number used throughout Revelation, is:
   a. Perfection
   b. Good fortune
   c. The church
   d. Satan's sign
   e. A sign of the end of the world

Write the number of EACH symbol on the blank in front of the ONE term which best gives the symbol's meaning. Do this for both groups. In the first group, use ONE or MORE numbers more than once. One term has TWO numbers.

_____ Hades	1.	Seven lampstands
_____ Churches	2.	Being with sword in mouth
_____ Prayers of God's people	3.	Seven stars
_____ Rome	4.	Gold bowls of incense
_____ Spirits of God	5.	Seven torches
_____ Angels of the churches	6.	Babylon
_____ Locusts	7.	Plagues
_____ Jesus Christ	8.	Lamb

_____ Twelve tribes of Israel	1.	Stones
_____ Witnesses of God's message	2.	Prostitute
_____ Eternal life	3.	Two trees by stream
_____ Christ	4.	Lake of fire
_____ Last plagues	5.	Gates
_____ Rome	6.	Seven bowls
_____ Second death	7.	Two lamps and olive trees
_____ Twelve apostles	8.	Rider of white horse

Circle the numbers of five distinguishing features of Revelation.
1. Apocalyptic style
2. Proverbial style
3. Numerology
4. Rhetorical questions
5. Visions
6. Symbolism
7. Warnings against immorality
8. Greek mystical themes
9. Resistance in persecution
10. Instructions for leaders

Check answers on page 86 and compute scores below.

PRE-TEST SCORES

Category	# Correct	% Score	Directions
A. Structure	_____	_____	# x 20 = %
B. Narratives	_____	_____	# x 5 = %
C. Features	_____	_____	# x 4 = %
Total (A+B+C)	_____	_____	# x 2 = %

Enter ALL percent scores on the Unit 2 Growth Record on page 90.
Then begin the study of Revelation on the next page.

UNIT 2: THE REVELATION OF JOHN

The book of Revelation is the only book in the New
Testament which is an APOCALYPSE, a common Jewish
literary form popular at this period.

The subject matter of an apocalypse is always
ESCHATOLOGICAL (concerning the end of the world). In
Mark's Little Apocalypse, with parallels in Matthew
and Luke, Jesus gives an eschatological discourse.

The apocalyptic writer usually reports what he learned
from visions, and the writing abounds in SYMBOLISM.
To the modern Western eye, it is strange and almost
incomprehensible. Even with the help of teachers and
scholars the reader must make a real effort to appreciate
the beauty and strength in the message of God's
sovereignty. It is not the purpose of this program
to give such interpretative assistance, so the reader may
want to investigate other sources for further study.

Descriptions of visions, use of symbolism (especially numbers, animals,
and colors), and a distinctive view of world history all characterize the
Revelation to John as apocalyptic. The strong imagery not only increases
the force of the message, but was used to protect the writer in a time of
persecution. Some of the more common symbols used are:

seven = perfection	red = war	lamb = sacrifice
twelve = God's redeemed	white = triumph	lion = strength

An interpretation agreed upon by most Christians is that the BABYLON described in Revelation was its counterpart at the time of
writing: Rome, the city built on seven hills.

Although Unit 2 treats only one New Testament book, it has been divided into
four sections of guided reading so you will have less material to learn at
one time.

BACKGROUND OF REVELATION

AUTHOR: A Jewish-Christian prophet named John (1:1, 4, 9). The tradition
   that he is John the apostle, son of Zebedee, is questioned by
   many scholars.
SITUATION and DATE: Probably during the persecution of Christians under
   Domitian, ca. A.D. 90-95.
PURPOSE: To encourage Christians of the Roman province of Asia to resistance
   and perseverance.
LITERARY FORM: Apocalypse. Its alternative title is "The Apocalypse of
   John."

60

11   PROLOGUE. READ: Revelation 1:1-3

Why did Jesus Christ send his angel to John to reveal the things
written in this book?

12   LETTERS: Chs. 1-3

12A Authorized by Christ. READ: Revelation 1:4-20

1.   To whom was John writing?

                 ****

21   APOCALYPSE PROPER: HEAVEN, EARTH, AND GOD'S PEOPLE: Chs. 4-11
     READ: Revelation 4--5

21A The Throne and the Lamb

1.   John was shown the next visions so he would know what would be happening
     on earth. What do the seven torches represent?

2.   What did the 24 elders and the 4 creatures do?

                 ****

31   THE DRAGON, LAST PLAGUES, AND BABYLON: 12:1--19:10

31A The Dragon, the Redeemed, and the Harvest. READ: Revelation 12--14

1.   The woman's son would some day rule all nations with an iron rod.
     After Michael defeated the dragon, what happened to the dragon
     and his angels?

2.   When the woman was saved from the dragon, what did he do?

3.   The beast of the sea got his authority from the dragon for 42 months.
     Who worshiped the beast and against whom did it fight?

                 ****

41   THE RETURN OF CHRIST: 19:11--22:17

41A The End. READ: 19:11--20:15

1.   What three names were given the rider of the white horse? (You may
     want to note all the clues that he is Jesus Christ.)

11

To show God's servants what
would happen very soon

12A

1.   To the seven churches in
     the province of Asia

****

21A

1.   The spirits of God

2.   They worshiped God.

****

31A

1.   He was thrown down to earth
     as Satan to deceive the world.

2.   Went off to fight against her
     descendants, those who obey God

3.   It fought against God's people,
     and all other people worshiped it.

****

41A

1.   Faithful and True
     The Word of God
     King of kings and
         Lord of lords

12A Letters Authorized by Christ: 1:4-20

2. John was writing from Patmos (an island west of Miletus). Why was he writing from there?

3. Who spoke to John, telling him not to be afraid?

4. What do the lampstands and stars represent?

****

21A The Throne and the Lamb: Chs. 4-5

3. The worthy one is described as two animals. What are they?

4. What are the gold bowls of incense?

5. Who praised the Father and the Son?

****

31A The Dragon, the Redeemed, and the Harvest: Chs. 12-14

4. What did the beast out of the earth do? What else was he called?

5. Who were the pure men who were the first to be redeemed?

6. What was the warning of the third angel?

7. What happened at harvesttime?

****

41A The End: 19:11--20:15

2. What happened to the beast and the false prophet after they were captured?

3. After the dragon was thrown into the abyss and locked up for a thousand years, who were first raised from the dead and what did they do?

12A

2. He had been imprisoned
   there for proclaiming
   God's word.

3. Christ: dead but now alive,
   authority over death (later
   called Son of God)

4. The seven churches and their
   angels

****

21A

3. The lion of Judah and the lamb

4. The prayers of God's people

5. All creation

****

31A

4. Called False Prophet, he performed
   great miracles, forced people to
   worship image of first beast, and to
   bear the beast's mark, 666.

5. The 144,000

6. Those who worshiped the beast would
   be tormented forever.

7. One angel reaped the harvest on
   earth and another threw grapes
   into the winepress of God's anger.

****

41A

2. They were thrown into the lake of fire.

3. Martyrs lived again and
   ruled with Christ for 1,000 years.

12B Letters to the Seven Churches: Chs. 2-3

    READ: Revelation 2

1. What would those at Ephesus who won the victory receive?

2. Concerning the letter to Smyrna, how would the Devil put the Christians there to the test? What would the faithful receive?

            ****

21B The Seven Seals. READ: Revelation 6:1--8:5

1. The rider (conquest) who appeared after the first seal was broken was prepared to be the conqueror. What power did the second rider have?

2. The third rider (famine) spoke of what would be a whole day's wages. Who followed the fourth rider and what could he and the rider do?

3. The souls of martyrs appeared after the opening of the fifth seal. How long were they told to rest?

            ****

31B The Seven Bowls. READ: Revelation 15--16

1. The seven angels had the last plagues in seven bowls. What did these plagues express?

2. When the first bowl was poured out, what plague appeared on earth?

3. What happened when the second and third bowls were poured?

            ****

41A The End: 19:11--20:15

4. How would Satan finally be destroyed at the end of this period?

5. When all the dead stood before the throne, and the book of the living was opened, how were the people judged?

12B

1. The right to eat of the fruit of the tree of life

2. Some would be thrown in prison, and troubles would last ten days. The faithful would receive the crown of life.

```
**********************************
```

21B

1. To bring war

2. Hades and the rider, Death, could kill one-fourth of the earth.

3. Until the total number of martyrs was reached

```
**********************************
```

31B

1. They were the final expression of God's wrath.

2. Painful sores on those who had the mark of the beast

3. The sea, rivers, and springs turned into blood.

```
**********************************
```

41A

4. After being loosed and trying to deceive the nations, he would be thrown into the lake of fire.

5. According to what they had done as written in the books

Fill in blanks 1-4 on Section Chart 4, page 80. Check answers on page 77 and study corrected chart. Then continue on page 67.

12B Letters to the Seven Churches: Chs. 2-3

3. How had the people in the church at Pergamum displeased God?
    What would those who won the victory receive?

4. What would those at Thyatira who won the victory receive?

                ****

21B The Seven Seals: 6:1--8:5

4. After the sixth seal was opened there were many unnatural upheavals.
    What did the men on earth do?

5. What happened to the 144,000?

6. Who were the people in the great crowd?

7. What happened when the lamb broke open the seventh seal?

                ****

31B The Seven Bowls: Chs. 15-16

4. After the fourth and fifth bowls, men were burned and in pain.
    How did they act then?

5. Where did the kings assemble for battle after the sixth bowl?

6. What was the seventh plague of the bowls?

                ****

JUST FOR FUN!!

The battle of Armageddon referred to in ch. 16 is described in detail in
ch. 19. Remembering the purpose of this book (to encourage those suffering
persecution) and also the meaning of some of the symbols, you may want to
consider the ways in which the writer encouraged his readers in this section.

Do you think he intended the Christian to take pleasure in the torture of
the Emperor and the Roman soldiers? In what ways can you interpret this
story to see it as inspiring and helpful to the Christian both then and
today?

12B

3. Some had followed false teachers
    and committed immorality. The
    faithful would receive hidden
    manna and a new name.

4. The morning star and authority
    to rule over nations

****

21B

4. Hid in caves from the lamb's wrath

5. They were marked with God's seal.

6. From every nation and people, those
    who had come safely through the
    persecution

7. A half hour of silence in heaven,
    then the angels were given trumpets

Fill in blanks 1-7 on Section Chart 2, page 78. Check answers on page 77
and continue on page 69.

Fill in blanks 1-7 on Section Chart 2, page 78. Check answers on page 77
and continue on page 69.

****

31B

4. The same as before--
    they did not repent.

5. Armageddon

6. Great hailstones

Fill in blanks 1-8 on Section Chart 3, page 79. Check answers on page 77.
Then turn to page 69.

Fill in blanks 1-8 on Section Chart 3, page 79. Check answers on page 77.
Then turn to page 69.

****

JUST FOR FUN!!
See if you can identify six characters from Revelation. They have been hidden
in sentences as Revelation has been hidden in the example.
Ex.: Easter Eve Lat, Iona born, showed slides of Scotland.
1. He advocated law, order, and peace.
2. The stick has a red rag on the end.
3. O.K., Smarty! Race me home.
4. He left his robe astern.
5. You saw Miles at an opera!
6. Judaism and Islam bring conflicting ideas.

6. Lamb
5. Satan
4. Beast
3. Martyr
2. Dragon
1. Word

JUST FOR FUN!!

As you started reading, you probably remembered that Revelation contains the apocalyptic writing popular in Judaism at that time. A little practice in using it may prove fun and also give you a better feel for the rest of Revelation. First try to "translate" this sentence:

> From alpha, four lions had white manes.
> (From the beginning, on earth, strength triumphed.)

Make up a story, representing history or abstract concepts, using apocalyptic symbols. You may refer to books on apocalyptic writing or use the few symbols on the next page.

****

JUST FOR FUN!!

In Section 1 you practiced using some of the symbolism so meaningful to the Jewish Christians. Perhaps you would like to try out some symbolism which would be meaningful to you.

John gives a vivid picture of heaven and explains some of his symbols. What is your idea of heaven? Try expressing your ideas in symbols which have meaning today, or at least to you. If you like to draw, a sketch may be in order.

****

JUST FOR FUN!!

The kingdom of the dragon and the mark of the beast have been identified as different specific men and symbols throughout the ages. John's saying that 666 is a man's name is an application of the system of gematria. In this each letter had a certain mathematical equivalent, and a man's worth was determined by adding up the letters of his name.

Maybe you'd like to determine your "worth" and perhaps "predict" the outcome of the next election! See the code and the examples on the next page.

****

41B The New Creation.   READ: Revelation 21--22

1.   What would be new about God's relationship with man?

2.   What was the second death?

JUST FOR FUN!!

Numbers	Colors	Animals	Words
7 = perfection	white = triumph	lion = strength	alpha = first or beginning
6 = less than perfect, or man's affairs	black = famine	lamb = sacrifice	omega = last or ending
4 = earth	red = fighting		
3 = spiritual world	green = eternal life		
(Note: 3 + 4 = 7			

****

JUST FOR FUN!!

Some scholars and artists have thought that the four living creatures represented the four Gospel writers--Matthew with the head of a lion, Luke with the head of a calf, Mark with the head of a man, and John with the head of an eagle. Reviewing what you know about each of these men and these symbols, see if you can determine why these associations were made. (For instance, three men were Jewish and three symbols were animals.)

****

JUST FOR FUN!!   An Adaptation of Gematria to English

a = 1	k = 10	t = 100
b = 2	l = 20	u = 200
c = 3	m = 30	v = 300
d = 4	n = 40	w/x = 400
e = 5	o = 50	y = 500
f = 6	p = 60	z = 600
g = 7	q = 70	
h = 8	r = 80	
i/j = 9	s = 90	

John Brown = 679
Mary Smith = 848

Greek letters (like Latin and Hebrew) were used for computation. The first nine letters were given the values 1-9. The second nine letters were given the values 10-90, and the last letters valued in the hundreds. There was no J, Q, or W, but xi came between n and o, so Q substitutes for xi in this table.

****

41B

1.   God's home would then be with man. He would allow no more pain or death.

2.   The lake of fire

12B Letters to the Seven Churches. READ: Revelation 3

5.   Concerning the letter to Sardis, what was wrong with the fellowship
     there? What were the people told to do? What would those who won
     the victory receive?

             ****

21C The Seven Trumpets and Two Witnesses: 8:6--11:19
     READ: Revelation 8:6--9:21

1.   Hail, fire, and blood burned a third of the earth. What destroyed
     a third of sea life and other waters?

2.   After a third of the natural light was gone, what did the eagle
     announce?

3.   After the fifth trumpet, what came out of the abyss and who was
     harmed?

4.   After the angels killed a third of mankind by fire (the sixth
     trumpet), how did the rest of mankind act?

             ****

31C The Fall of Babylon. READ: Revelation 17:1--19:10

1.   What was the name of the prostitute and what made her drunk?

2.   What was the meaning of the dead one once alive who would
     reappear?

             ****

41B The New Creation. Chs. 21-22

3.   Who was the bride of the lamb?

4.   What were on the twelve gates? On the twelve stones?

12B

5. They were dead.
   They should wake up, obey, and turn
   from their sins.
   Their names would be left in the
   book of the living.

****

21C

1. A large burning mountain turned
   a third of the sea into blood,
   and a large burning star fell on
   a third of the rivers and springs,
   making them poisonous for drinking.

2. The horrors to come with the next
   three trumpets

3. Locusts with the power of scorpions
   came out and harmed only the men
   who were not marked by God's seal.

4. The same; they did not repent.

****

31C

1. The great Babylon (Rome) was drunk
   on the blood of God's people.

2. A king of Rome (seven hills on which
   "the woman" sits), the eighth in a series

****

41B

3. The new Jerusalem

4. Names of the twelve tribes of Israel
   Names of the twelve apostles

12B Letters to the Seven Churches: Chs. 2-3

6. What would happen to the victorious in the church at
    Philadelphia?

             ****

21C The Seven Trumpets and Two Witnesses: 8:6--11:19
     READ: Revelation 10--11

5. Seven thunders answered the angel with the small scroll.
    What was John told to do with the scroll? With the measuring stick?

             ****

31C The Fall of Babylon: 17:1--19:10

3. Who was the woman?

4. After the angel announced the fall of Babylon (Rome), why did he
    say Babylon would be punished?

             ****

41B The New Creation: Chs. 21-22

5. What lighted the city?

6. Where would the tree of life grow?

12B

6. They would become pillars in the temple of God and stay there forever. Christ would write on them his new name.

****

21C

5. To eat the scroll; to measure the temple

****

31C

3. The city that dominated the kings of the earth (Rome)

4. Because the blood of the prophets and of God's people was found in the city

****

41B

5. The glory of God and the lamp of the lamb

6. On either side of the river of life

12B Letters to the Seven Churches: Chs. 2-3

7.   What did the letter to Laodicea criticize concerning that group of Christians? What would the victorious receive?

            ****

21C The Seven Trumpets and Two Witnesses: 8:6--11:19

6.   What would happen to the two witnesses after they gave their message?

7.   What would happen after the seventh trumpet?

            ****

31C The Fall of Babylon: 17:1--19:10

5.   What three groups mourned the fall of Babylon?

6.   What did the great crowd of people in heaven say?

7.   This triumph was celebrated in heaven by what great feast?

            ****

41B The New Creation: Chs. 21-22

7.   After Jesus said, "I am coming soon," what did he want his listeners to accept?

42   CONCLUSION: 22:18-21

12B

7. For being barely warm;
   the right to sit by Christ
   on his throne

Now complete blanks 1-10 on Section Chart 1, page 77. After checking answers and studying corrected chart, take Section Test 1, page 81.

****

21C

6. After being killed by the beast,
   their bodies would be left in
   the street for 3½ days. Then
   they would be brought to life
   and be taken into heaven.

7. God would rule.

Now complete Section Chart 2 on page 78. Check answers on page 77, study chart, and take Section Test 2 on page 82.

****

31C

5. The kings of the earth, the
   businessmen, and the seafarers

6. "Praise God!"

7. The wedding of the lamb

Now turn to Section Chart 3, page 79, to complete the blanks. Check your answers on page 77 and study the chart. Then take Section Test 3, page 83.

****

41B

7. The water of life as a gift

Now complete Section Chart 4, page 80. Check your answers on page 77 and study the chart. Then take Section Test 4, page 84.

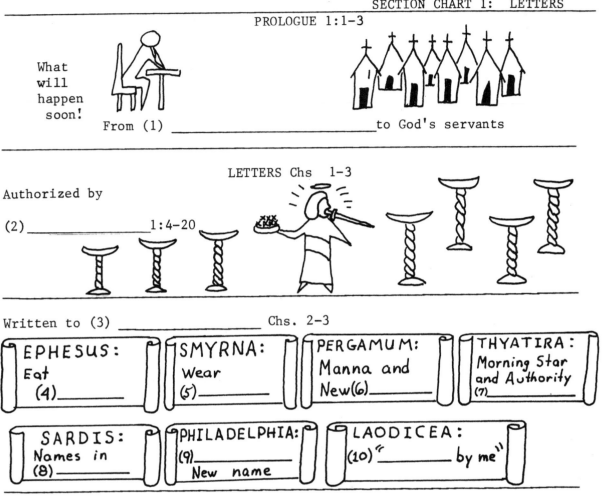

PROLOGUE 1:1-3

What
will
happen
soon!

From (1) _____ to God's servants

LETTERS Chs 1-3

Authorized by

(2) _____ 1:4-20

Written to (3) _____ Chs. 2-3

EPHESUS:
Eat
(4)_____

SMYRNA:
Wear
(5)_____

PERGAMUM:
Manna and
New(6)_____

THYATIRA:
Morning Star
and Authority
(7)_____

SARDIS:
Names in
(8)_____

PHILADELPHIA:
(9)_____
New name

LAODICEA:
(10) "_____ by me"

Check answers below and study corrected chart.

ANSWERS TO SECTION CHARTS

Sect. 1	Sect. 2	Sect. 3	Sect. 4
1. John	1. Elders	1. Michael	1. End
2. Christ	2. Creatures	2. Beast	2. 1,000
3. 7 churches	3. Torches	3. 666	3. Martyrs
4. Fruit of tree	4. Seals	4. Redeemed	4. Deceive
of life	5. War	5. Bowls	5. Creation
5. Crown of life	6. Lamb's	6. Sores	6. Bride
6. Name	wrath	7. Repentance	7. Apostles
7. To rule	7. Sealing	8. Armageddon	8. Lighted
8. Book of Living	8. Trumpets	9. Fall	9. Coming
nations	9. Witnesses	10. Prostitute	10. Water
9. Christ's	10. Rules	11. Wedding	
10. Sit			

SECTION CHART 2: APOCALYPSE PROPER

HEAVEN, EARTH, AND GOD'S PEOPLE

THE THRONE Ch. 4   THE LAMB Ch. 5

24 (1) _____

4 living
(2) _____
7 (3) _____

Worthy One

THE SEVEN (4) _____ 6:1--8:5

1. Conquest   2. (5) _____   3. Wages (famine)   4. Death

5. Martyrs   6. Hiding from   (7) _____   7. Silence
                          (6) _____   God's people

THE SEVEN (8) _____ 8:6--11:19

1. Hail - Fire   2. Burning mountain   Bitter
                          killed sea life.   water

                                                              4.

                      6. One third
                          of men killed

                                          SCROLL

5. Stinging and pain

                                          The two (9) _____

        7. The Lord (10) _____!

Check answers on page 77. Then study corrected chart.

THE DRAGON, LAST PLAGUES, AND BABYLON
THE DRAGON, THE REDEEMED, AND THE HARVEST Chs. 12-14

Son
  to rule
  all nations

Defeated by (1) _____
Beast out of the earth

(2) _____ out of the sea

Mark of
the beast (3) _____

144,000: The first (4) _____

The Harvest

THE SEVEN (5) _____ Chs. 15-16
                              Final expression
                  Last   of God's wrath
                  Plagues

1
Painful
(6) ____

2   3
Seas   Water
   Blood

4   5
Burns   Pains

6
Kings at
(8) _____

But no
(7) _____

7
Hailstones

(9) _____ OF BABYLON 17:1--19:10

Drunk
(10) _____

Babylon has fallen!

Blood of
God's
People

Heaven: Praise God!
The (11) _____ of the lamb

Check answers on page 77 and study corrected chart.

SECTION CHART 4:   APOCALYPSE PROPER
                        THE RETURN OF CHRIST
                THE (1) _____ 19:11--20:15
KING OF KINGS   (2) _____ YEARS

Beast

False
Prophet

Satan

(3) _____ rule
with Christ

SATAN

FINAL JUDGMENT:

Loosed

In book of living
                                    with
Not in book of living   God

Tried to (4) _____,

Thrown into

THE NEW (5) _____ Chs. 21-22

NEW RELATIONSHIP:

NEW

HEAVEN

NEW

EARTH

HOLY CITY: (6) _____

Gates: 12 tribes
Stones: 12 (7) _____

(8) _____ by

God's

Glory

No
Death

God
and
Man

No
Pain

LIFE

I AM (9) _____ SOON

Accept the (10) _____ of life

CONCLUSION 22:18-21

Check answers on page 77 and study corrected chart.

SECTION TEST 1: LETTERS

A. STRUCTURE. Fill in the blanks of this outline of Section 1.

(1) _____: From John to God's people

I. (2) _____

    A. (3) _____ by _____

    B. (4) _____ to _____

B. NARRATIVES. Write the number of a person, group, or place on the blank before the phrase with which it is most closely associated. Use TWO numbers TWICE. DO NOT use TWO numbers at all.

_____ Province of the seven churches
_____ Revealed the future to John
_____ Writer of Revelation
_____ Where John was imprisoned
_____ "I am the first and the last."
_____ Rewards for the victorious
_____ Saw vision of Christ

1. John
2. Jesus
3. Seven churches
4. Martyrs
5. Asia
6. Macedonia
7. Patmos

C. FEATURES. On the blank before each symbol write the number of the ONE term which gives its meaning. DO NOT use TWO numbers.

_____ Seven gold lampstands
_____ Seven stars
_____ Being with sword in mouth

1. Angel of God
2. Churches
3. Jesus Christ
4. God's redeemed
5. Angels of the churches

Check answers on page 86 and compute scores below.

SECTION TEST 1 SCORES

Category	# Correct	% Scores	Directions
A. Structure	_____	_____	# x 25 = %
B. Narratives	_____	_____	See chart, p. 83, for 7 #.
C. Features	_____	_____	# x 33 = ___ + 1 = %
Total (A+B+C)	_____	_____	See chart, p. 83, for 14 #.

Enter ALL percent scores on Unit 2 Growth Record, page 90. Then review material for any items missed and begin Section 2 on page 61.

SECTION TEST 2: THE APOCALYPSE PROPER
HEAVEN, EARTH, AND GOD'S PEOPLE

A. STRUCTURE. Fill in the blanks of this outline of Section 2.

II. (1) _____ Proper

    A. Heaven, Earth, and God's People
       1. The (2) _____ and the _____

       2. The (3) _____

       3. The (4) _____ and Two _____

B. NARRATIVES. In each group write the number of EACH person, animal, or
    object on the blank before the ONE phrase with which it is most closely
    associated. ONE blank has TWO numbers.

____	Lion of Judah and lamb	1. 24 elders
____	Announced future horrors	2. 4 creatures
____	Praised God	3. Worthy one
____	Worshiped God	4. All creatures
		5. Eagle
____	Bodies in street 3½ days	6. Angels
____	Harmed those without God's seal	7. Locusts
____	Measured temple	8. John
____	Given trumpets	9. Great crowd
____	Those who came through the	10. Two witnesses
	persecution	

C. FEATURES. Write on the blank, before both the torches and the bowls,
    the number of the ONE phrase with which each symbol is most closely
    associated. Do NOT use TWO numbers.

____	Seven torches	1. Church
____	Gold bowls of incense	2. God's wrath
		3. Spirits of God
		4. Prayers of God's people

Circle the numbers of FOUR terms associated with what followed any seal
or trumpet.

1. Famine	5. Apostles
2. Thunder and lightning	6. Floods
3. Souls of Martyrs	7. Locusts
4. Hades and death	8. Wild beasts

Check answers on page 86 and compute scores on page 83. Then enter ALL percent
scores on the Unit 2 Growth Record, page 90. Review material for items missed,
then turn to page 61 to begin the study of Section 3.

SECTION TEST 2 SCORES

Category	# Correct	% Scores	Directions
A. Structure	_____	_____	# x 25 = %
B. Narratives	_____	_____	# x 10 = %
C. Features	_____	_____	See chart below for 6 #.
Total (A+B+C)	_____	_____	# x 5 = %

- % Conversion Charts

#	1	2	3	4	5	6	#
%	17	33	50	67	83	100	%

#	1	2	3	4	5	6	7	#
%	14	29	43	57	71	86	100	%

#	1	2	3	4	5	6	7	8	9	#
%	11	22	33	44	56	67	78	89	100	%

#	1	2	3	4	5	6	7	8	9	10	11	#
%	9	18	27	36	45	55	64	73	82	91	100	%

#	1	2	3	4	5	6	7	8	9	10	11	12	13	14	#
%	7	14	21	29	36	43	50	57	64	71	79	86	93	100	%

SECTION TEST 3: THE APOCALYPSE PROPER
THE DRAGON, LAST PLAGUES, AND BABYLON

A.   STRUCTURE. Fill in the blanks of the outline of Section 3.

II.   The Apocalypse Proper

    B.   The Dragon, Last Plagues, and (1) _____

        1.   The (2) _____, the Redeemed, and the _____

        2.   The (3) _____

        3.   The (4) _____ of _____

B.   NARRATIVES. Write the number of EACH person or animal on the blank
before the phrase with which it is most closely associated.

_____ Thrown to earth as Satan   1. Woman's son
_____ To rule with iron rod   2. Michael
_____ Forced all men to wear   3. Dragon
       mark of beast   4. Beast of the sea
_____ Defeated dragon   5. Beast of the earth
_____ Worshiped by the people

Match these groups, places, or occasions in the same way as you did the first group. Do NOT use ONE number.

____ Kings, businessmen, seafarers   6. First redeemed
____ Where kings assembled for battle   7. Armageddon
____ Heaven praised God   8. Mourners
____ 144,000 pure men   9. Wedding of lamb
                                                       10. City of seven hills

C.   FEATURES. Write the number of EACH symbol on the blank before the phrase with which it is most closely associated. ONE symbol will be used TWICE. ONE phrase will have TWO numbers.

____ Rome   1. 666
____ God's wrath   2. Seven bowls
____ Witnesses who proclaim   3. Prostitute
      God's message   4. Dead one who will
____ Mark of the beast, a   reappear
      man's name   5. Babylon
____ Eighth king of Rome   6. Two lamps and two
____ Seven last plagues   olive trees

Check answers on page 86 and compute scores below. Enter ALL percent scores on Unit 2 Growth Record, page 90. Review material for items missed and begin the study of Section 4 on page 61.

SECTION TEST 3 SCORES

Category	# Correct	% Scores	Directions
A. Structure	____	____	# x 25 = %
B. Narratives	____	____	See chart, p. 83, for 9 #.
C. Features	____	____	See chart, p. 83, for 7 #.
Total (A+B+C)	____	____	# x 5 = %

SECTION TEST 4: THE APOCALYPSE PROPER
THE RETURN OF CHRIST

A.   STRUCTURE. Fill in the blanks of this outline of Section 4.

II. The Apocalypse Proper

    C. The (1) _____ of (2) _____

        1. The (3) _____

        2. The New (4) _____

    Conclusion

B. NARRATIVES. On EACH blank write the ONE number of the person(s) or
    object with which it is most closely associated. (In the first group
    use one or more numbers MORE than once. Do NOT use TWO numbers at all.)

_____ Faithful and True   1. Rider of white horse
_____ Ruled for 1,000 years with Christ   2. Dragon
_____ Actions written in books   3. 144,000 Israelites
_____ King of kings   4. Final judgment
_____ Locked up for 1,000 years 5. Beast from the sea
_____ Word of God   6. Martyrs

Use EACH number ONCE:

_____ God's new home with man   1. Jesus
_____ Gift of Jesus   2. Bride of the lamb
_____ Returning soon   3. No death, no pain
_____ Source of city's light   4. Glory of God
_____ New Jerusalem   5. Water of life

C. FEATURES. Write ONE number on the blank before EACH of the following
    symbols. Do NOT use FIVE numbers.

_____ Rider of the white horse   1. Source of Satan's power
_____ Lake of fire   2. Twelve apostles
_____ Two trees by river   3. Jesus
_____ Gates   4. Entrance to heaven and hell
_____ Stones   5. King of Rome
                                 6. Tribes of Israel
                                 7. Witnesses
                                 8. Man's oppression
                                 9. Second death
                                10. Eternal life

Check answers on page 86 and compute scores below.

SECTION TEST 4 SCORES

Category	# Correct	% Scores	Directions
A. Structure	_____	_____	# x 25 = %
B. Narratives	_____	_____	See chart, p. 83, for 11#.
C. Features	_____	_____	# x 20 = %
Total (A+B+C)	_____	_____	# x 5 = %

Enter ALL percent scores on Unit 2 Growth Record, page 90. Study material for
items missed and then take Unit Test 2, page 87.

ANSWERS TO PRE-TEST FOR UNIT 2

A. STRUCTURE (5)

1. b   2
2. c   3
3. e

B. NARRATIVES (20)

4	1	2	4
7	6	4	3
9	5	5	1
3	2	3	5
8		1	2
10			

C. FEATURES (25)

			7	7	5	4	1
1. d	1	2,8			7	1	3
2. b	4				3		5
3. a	6				8		6
	5				6		9
	3				2		

ANSWERS TO SECTION TESTS FOR UNIT 2

Sect. 1

A. STRUCTURE (4)

1. Prologue
2. Letters
3. Authorized by Christ
4. Written to the Seven
   Churches

B. NARRATIVES (7)

5
2
1
7
2
3
1

C. FEATURES (3)

2
5
3

Sect. 2

A. STRUCTURE (4)

1. Apocalypse
2. Throne and the Lamb
3. Seven Seals
4. Seven Trumpets and Witnesses

B. NARRATIVES (10)

3	10
5	7
4	8
1,2	6
	9

C. FEATURES (6)

3	1
4	3
	4
	7

Sect. 3

A. STRUCTURE (4)

1. Babylon
2. The Dragon, the Redeemed,
   and the Harvest
3. The Seven Bowls
4. The Fall of Babylon

B. NARRATIVES (9)

3	8
1	7
5	9
2	6
4	

C. FEATURES (7)

3, 5
2
6
1
4
2

Sect. 4

A. STRUCTURE (4)

1. Return
2. Christ
3. End
4. Creation

B. NARRATIVES (11)

1	3
6	5
4	1
1	4
2	2
1	

C. FEATURES (5)

3
9
10
6
2

UNIT TEST 2:   REVELATION

A.   STRUCTURE. Fill in the blanks of the outline of Revelation.

Prologue

I.   (1)_____

   A.   Authorized by Vision of Christ

   B.   Written to the (2) _____

II.   (3) _____

   A.   Heaven, Earth, and God's People

      1.   The Throne and the Lamb

      2.   The (4) _____

      3.   The (5) _____

   B.   The Dragon, Last Plagues, and Babylon

      1.   The (6) _____, the Redeemed, and the _____

      2.   The (7) _____

      3.   The (8) _____ of _____

   C.   The (9) _____ of _____

      1.   The End

      2.   The New (10) _____

B.   NARRATIVES. Circle the letter of the ONE BEST answer.

1.   John was writing from the island of Patmos because:
   a.   He was head of the church there.
   b.   He was visiting the church on a missionary journey.
   c.   He had been shipwrecked.
   d.   He was in prison for preaching the gospel.
   e.   It was his home.

2.   All the letters to the churches included:
   a.   The good things the members had done
   b.   How they had pleased God
   c.   The sins they should turn from
   d.   How they would be tested
   e.   The reward which the victorious would receive

3. The only one found worthy to open the seals was:
   a. The six-winged creature
   b. The lamb
   c. The one on the throne
   d. The angel
   e. John

4. At the battle of Armageddon:
   a. The angels fought against Satan.
   b. The kings of the earth fought against Christ.
   c. The beast of the sea attacked the lamb.
   d. The rider of the white horse triumphed over the kings of the earth.
   e. b and d

Write the number of EACH man or animal on the blank before the ONE term with which it is most closely associated.

_____ To rule with an iron rod	1.	John
_____ Defeated the dragon	2.	Woman's son
_____ King of kings	3.	Dragon
_____ Measured temple	4.	Rider of white horse
_____ The new Jerusalem	5.	Bride of the lamb
_____ Announced coming horrors	6.	Beast of the sea
_____ Locked up for 1,000 years	7.	Michael
_____ Worshiped by the people	8.	Eagle

Write the number of EACH group or place on the blank before the ONE term with which it is most closely associated.

_____ 144,000	1.	Martyrs
_____ Kings, businessmen, seafarers	2.	The first redeemed
_____ Rule for 1,000 years	3.	Great crowd
_____ Those who come through the persecution	4.	Mourners
_____ City of hills and kings	5.	Asia
_____ Province of seven churches	6.	Patmos
_____ Kings assembled here for final battle.	7.	Armageddon
_____ Where John was imprisoned	8.	Rome

C. FEATURES. Identify EACH of the following symbols in each of the two groups by writing its number on the blank before the ONE term which most adequately gives its meaning. Use ONE symbol TWICE.

____ Spirits of God	1. Seven gold lampstands	
____ Rome	2. Seven stars	
____ Mark of the beast	3. Seven torches	
____ Hailstones	4. Gold bowls of incense	
____ Churches	5. Plagues	
____ Hades and death	6. 666	
____ Angels of the churches	7. Babylon	
____ Prayers of God's people		

____ Second death	1. Prostitute	
____ Tribes of Israel	2. Seven bowls	
____ Last plagues	3. Two lamps and olive trees	
____ Apostles	4. Rider of white horse	
____ Jesus	5. Lake of fire	
____ Eternal life	6. Two trees by river	
____ Rome	7. Gates	
____ Witnesses of God's message	8. Stones	

Circle the numbers of FOUR items which are distinguishing features of Revelation.

1. Jewish proverbial style
2. Apocalyptic writing
3. Written to a Greek church
4. Anonymous

5. Numerology
6. Visions
7. Vivid account of church life
8. Symbolism

Check answers on page 90 and compute scores below.

UNIT TEST 2 SCORES

Category	# Correct	% Score	Directions
A. Structure	_____	_____	# x 10 = %
B. Narratives	_____	_____	# x 5 = %
C. Features	_____	_____	# x 5 = %
Total (A+B+C)	_____	_____	# x 2 = %

Enter ALL percent scores on the Unit 2 Growth Record, page 90. Then compute growth in each area by subtracting pre-test scores from unit test scores. Check references for any items missed on unit test.

ANSWERS TO UNIT TEST 2

A. STRUCTURE (10)

1. Letters
2. Seven Churches   (Refer to guided reading headings
3. Apocalypse Proper   and charts for any errors.)
4. Seven Seals
5. Seven Trumpets
6. The Dragon; Harvest
7. Seven Bowls
8. Fall of Babylon
9. Return of Christ
10. Creation

B. NARRATIVES (20)

	Man or Animal	Group or Place
1. d (1:9)	2 (12:5)	2 (14:1-3)
2. e (2--3)	7 (12:7-8)	4 (18:9, 11, 17b-19)
3. b (5:5, 9)	4 (19:16)	1 (20:4)
4. e (19:11-19)	1 (11:1)	3 (7:9, 14b)
	5 (21:9-10)	
	8 (8:13)	8 (17:9, 18)
	3 (20:1-3)	5 (1:4)
	6 (13:12b)	7 (16:16)
		6 (1:9)

C. FEATURES (20)

Group 1	Group 2	Group 3
3 (4:5)	5 (21:8)	2 (Refer to
7 (p. 60)	7 (21:12)	5 page 60 for
6 (13:18b)	2 (16:1)	6 any errors.)
5 (16:21)	8 (21:14)	8
1 (1:20)	4 (19:11-16)	
5 (6:8)	6 (22:1-2)	
2 (1:20)	1 (17:1, 9, 18)	
4 (5:8)	3 (11:4)	

UNIT 2 GROWTH RECORD

Category	Pre.	Sect. 1	Sect. 2	Sect. 3	Sect. 4	Unit	Growth
Structure	%	%	%	%	%	%	%
Narratives							
Features							
Total							